Praise for Exp

Note: Until I have celebrity authors review my book, I am taking liberty with authors who are no longer with us and what they might have said, if they were here to read it. With all due respect, here is what they probably would have said;

"Finally, a book that extends beyond the written word. Express Lane to Success gets into your heart and provides a fool-proof system to create the action necessary for success."

-Abraham Lincoln
16th President of the United States

"Drive your vehicle faster with Express Lane to Success!"

-David Schwartz
Author "Magic of Thinking Big"

"Express Lane to Success combines the motivation, action, belief and network necessary for achievement. I loved it!"

-Dale Carnegie
Author "How to Win Friends & Influence People"

"Success, often elusive is firmly placed into your hands as you read this book and apply the knowledge and system available. Doug maps them out for you and holds you accountable."

-Marcus Aurelius
Roman Emperor

"Independent professionals often need a reminder of the accountability necessary for achievement. Express Lane to Success delivers everything you need to make it happen."

-Aristotle
Ancient Greek Philosopher

Express Lane to Success

How to Win at Everything

The world's first interactive book that holds you accountable to your goals

Doug Crowe

Disclaimer

Dedication

This book is dedicated to Juan Ramirez.
The most positive person I've ever known.
His influence will reverberate in the universe forever.

Table of Contents

Section II

~ Action ~

Section III

~ Interaction ~

Introduction

This book is not meant to be read.

If you simply "read" this book and take no action, you are deciding to put your future in the dumper.

"Wow, Doug! What a great opening for a motivational book!"

You may perceive that statement as a challenge, a threat or creative incentive to do more than simply read about success. Reading motivational and self-improvement books are an important part of success. Reading without making changes in your thoughts, habits, or associations will not lead you where you want to go or get you close to your true potential.

In 2010, Amazon.com listed over 226,045 choices for buying a "self help" book. With such a proliferation of resources on improving our health, wealth and self-esteem why are we poorer, fatter and generally less enthusiastic than we were a few years ago? Don't get me wrong. These books are great. I think I own about 972 of them.

Why are you reading this one? Didn't the first one work? How about the second? Do you think that inside these pages you will find the final inspirational message that will take you over the edge and give you the life of your dreams?

Not a chance.

You see, if it was simply a matter of words, go immediately to the appendix and you will see a list of books that have good content...in fact, some of the content of these books is far superior to this one. This book contains some great inspiration, also. I am going to give you hard-hitting stories of rags to riches, of obesity to health, of loneliness to love. This book may contain a new twist on a familiar concept that will be a spark of inspiration for you.

So what?

You've heard many of these stories before and you still haven't cracked the code to the life you truly want. You know, deep in your gut, that you have the potential to do better, but you haven't been able to win big yet. Why?

The premise of this book is that while you are on the right track, there are critical components of success that are missing from your formula. You may need:

New hope
New beliefs
New encouragement
New actions
New associations
A new plan...

The bottom line is that to get the permanent, new and improved results for yourself, you need to have a comprehensive plan. You need more than just some motivation or a goal planning worksheet. You need a total package. With this book and system, you will, for the FIRST time, have all the pieces of the puzzle on the table and get it done.

Permanently.

In your prior journey to success you've had at your disposal a large array of tools, talents and plans. Some worked a bit, others had no effect whatsoever. However, once the race starts, your tactics will change as quickly as the weather. You'll need to stick to a solid strategy that is unwavering as you weave in and around the pot holes and detours. The metaphors of a race are very appropriate.

You are in the race of your life.

You are on a journey to improve your wealth, health and/or relationships. This race puts you, the driver, in a vehicle (Your opportunity) and you have a road map (Plan) and a highway (Life). Who you put in the vehicle and take advice from is instrumental to your success (Family, friends and mentor). Previously, you've failed on one or more levels. This book and our system will give you not simply the road map, but ALL the tools, vehicle, maintenance and fuel you need to win in your life.

This time it is different.

This is an interactive book that works on an evolutionary concept of thought, action and accountability. You can certainly simply read this book. However the real power is located in the application of the complete system available to you.

This time you will be held accountable.

Summary:

Express Lane to Success is an interactive book that will engage you to read, react and interact. At the conclusion of each section you will read a fascinating story of success and strength. The conclusion to this story will ONLY be available online. (That's right…the book isn't complete-on purpose!)

After you finish each story, answer a few questions and create a profile. This profile will unveil your personality, characteristics, background and desires. This information confidentially creates the most amazing system for goal achievement and accountability you have ever known. After you complete the interaction you can receive:

1. Customized motivation book. Your first book is a customized story of "Your Life". This motivational book read like it was written by you-because it is!
2. Personalized workbook. You receive a "cliff notes" version of this book in a workbook format. Designed to be used as a daily journal, it keeps you on track.
3. Nag-O-Matic$^{tm.}$ A system of voicemail, text, email system that gives you daily doses of motivation, accountability, reminders and encouragement to defeat negative influences. 100% customized to your mission and personality.
4. Accountability partner. This partner will talk with you via phone approximately 10 minutes per week to give and get feedback on your progress. By being accountable and encouraging others, you truly "pay it forward."
5. FREE achiever's network. Your online achiever's network allows you to share and learn with other people from around the world.

This community of superstars will begin online and migrate to an offline "success club" in major cities across the world as the business/book grows. For those who create permanent change in their own life and are able to encourage others, opportunity exists to become the future leaders of regional and national Bexsi^{tm} fellowship.

Section I

~ Thought ~

"The happiness of your life depends upon the quality of your thoughts. Guard it accordingly and entertain no notions unsuitable to virtue"

~Marcus Aurelius
Roman Emperor

Chapter One

• • •

"Most failures are destined from the beginning. Not from poor planning, but from an early seed of doubt."

~Doug Crowe

• • •

Why nothing works...and how to change it all

There are deep issues that block all of us from achievement. If you are like most people, you've read a few books on success and perhaps even heard a highly trained or inspiring motivational speaker.

Why is it, that we feel so much better after that experience? Certainly, if the other 500 people sitting around me paid hundreds or even a few thousand dollars to attend an event, it must work, right? According to a recent research, motivational seminars, or attending weekend wealth boot camps lines the pockets of the promoters to the tune of over $800 million annually and results in a failure rate of over 92% of all participants.

92% failure rate!

How can a business succeed with over 92% of its customers not reaping the benefits promised? What if only 8% of airline flights arrived on time (Wait a minute...that might not be a good example) What if only 8% of flights actually arrived at all! The internet era has raised our awareness such as knowing the "real" price of a car and given the consumer increased power in sniffing out hype and scams. The self help industry continues to churn out an amazing $9 billion dollars in revenue each and every year yet people are fatter, poorer and more dissatisfied than ever.

The only way an entire industry is able to grow with such an atrocious failure rate is because the true product being sold isn't success. It is hope.

Selling hope and redemption is a much easier sale to make because a feeling is easier to deliver than the results from your education. Hope can be created with a well spoken word or two.

I can create an image of a pink elephant in your head and I am not even in the same room with you. The pink elephant you are trying so hard not to think about (but are) is being created in your brain by me at this very moment and I don't even know who you are. In fact, while you are trying to NOT think of that pink elephant, I am probably sipping a daiquiri on the beach under a palm tree listening to the comforting sounds of the ocean washing up on the beach, oblivious to your pain.

See how easy it is to plant an image (or two) in your brain? Hope is just like that. "You can do it," repeated enough times can change your belief. The problem is hope is temporary. Only habits that create fundamental shifts in belief are permanent. This book starts with hope. Your follow through with the interactive components will do the rest.

Change Your Mind

As you read this book, I will be planting more hope, inspiration, motivation and ideas into your brain. Instilling hope in your consciousness will be exceedingly simple. I am telling you in advance that as you read this book, you WILL FEEL better.

That's a good thing.

What you DO with those feelings is going to be our mutual goal. In your hands you have the necessary tools to take action, measure it and be held accountable like never before. Unlike most other self improvement books which attempt to stir you to action, I am going to give you a brain-dead simple opportunity to take that action and make permanent changes in your life!

I am going to share with you stories and lessons that will give you the "Can do" spirit and empower you to tackle any task you set your mind to.

After you finish reading chapter 10 and learn the secret to creating 2 EXTRA WEEKS a year, you are going feel better ecstatic.

When you commit, write and date your goals in chapter 5, you will feel better about your recent loss in the stock market. Why? Because when you get to chapter 11 you will realize the infinite secret of true wealth.

Reading stories of massive accomplishment in the face of adversity is motivational. Sharing ideas that create new products, opportunities and profits is empowering. Applying what you learn and living the results will cause a chain reaction that your family will appreciate. By applying the principles learned in every area of your life, your Express Lane to Success will spread to people whom you never even meet.

This book is not meant to be read.

Reading books is very enjoyable and information can be transferred through the reading of materials whether they are books, reports or papers. Having a teacher can help to dispense that information, absorb that information and even test you on the information. A teacher is a great way to learn if the knowledge has been retained by you in your short-term memory. But only experiential application of that knowledge has any real meaning, has any real depth, has any kind of real results whether they are short-term or long-term, that can actually make a difference in your life.

This book is not meant to be simply read.

How We Truly Learn

Oh, how I wish I would've had this book in my hands just a few years ago! Why? Because this book is not just written for you – it's written *with* you. You have an opportunity to not just read this book – you can also the author of it. While reading is the foundation for knowledge, unfortunately self-directed learning by simply reading has dismal success rates. You have in your hands more than a book. You have the power to engage words, thoughts, action, habits, and association to achieve. Now, for perhaps the first time in your life, you have EVERYTHING you need to succeed.

Education is a funny thing. Reading books is an activity that many people do less of after graduating high school or college. Those that continue to seek out knowledge do so at the expense of other activities. Every hour spent reading is an hour you are taking from another potential activity.

The materials you read, therefore, had better be worth it.

Attending classes through a school or continuing education is required for many professions. For the self-empowered individual, there is no standardized system of education for most of what people seek. Wouldn't it be wonderful if there was an accredited academy of success, weight loss, financial intelligence or creating perfect marriages?

Instead, we have three basic models for learning:

One-way communication: I talk – you listen. You read and retain 10% of that knowledge. Books are great for dispensing knowledge – they are known as one-way communication.

Two-way communication: I talk, you listen, you talk back, and we exchange information. We both retain only about 10% of what we heard because we're too busy talking to the other person.

Three-way communication: We talk, listen and have a

● ● ●

"There are three kinds of men; one that learns by reading, the few who learn by observation and the rest of them who have to pee on the electric fence for themselves."

~Will Rogers

● ● ●

tangible, experiential learning process. This process creates a three-dimensional reinforcement of knowledge and turns it into an experience which is retained not just mentally but physically as well.

In order for a person to **ACT** in a certain way, they must **BELIEVE** that that action will cause a **RESULT**. Not all beliefs are good, of course. I once believed that eating a jelly donut would make me happy! That action caused a temporary result, of course. Yuk! But the long term negative result outweighed (no pun intended) the short term pleasure from the donut.

Conversely, a positive, core belief in fitness and health would naturally produce actions which support a healthy lifestyle-right?

Wrong.

The evidence of knowledge, training, and information on health (finances, relationships, etc.) is convoluted in the information age. There are always two points of view. The only clarity a person can derive from all the ideas, strategies and knowledge is a PERSONAL victory in whatever they need help with. Gaining a personal victory in a lifetime of failure, disappointment or negative influence is often a losing battle.

Interestingly, in the example of weight loss, our desire for immediate action works against not only the process, but the belief system necessary to achieve the very goal we desire! With a flawed belief system, all the diet, exercise, tools, training and coaching in the world will not work. Without a properly aligned belief system, ANY goal is doomed for failure or worse; mediocrity.

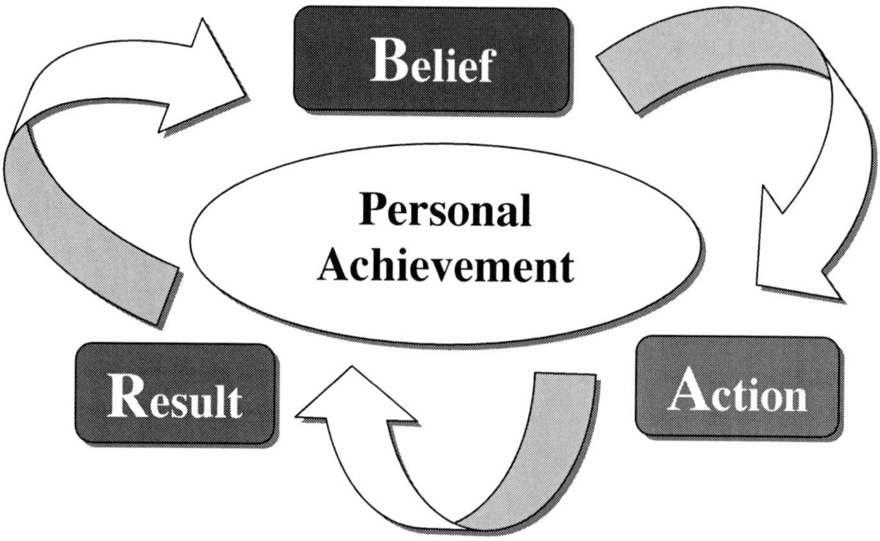

STEP 1: Belief

Without the RIGHT belief, a person's actions may not be congruent with the true result they desire. Misguided beliefs can spiral a goal down and create a lifetime of misery and disappointment. How many people have wasted their entire life and the lives of others with improperly channeled beliefs? Creating a new belief system along with the SUCCESS to support that belief is the mission.

If you TRULY believe that brushing your teeth daily delivers good oral hygiene (not to mention the ability to have friends), then you do it. Conversely, if you are a smoker, your belief is that smoking "isn't all that bad." Beliefs always precede any action.

STEP 2: Action

When a person takes action, they are energized because of the physical manifestation of their thoughts and beliefs. This empowers them because a result (negative or positive) occurs from their efforts. A system of correct action must be put forth and executed. People will not simply read our book, they will interact with themselves, the author and a private mentor who has the belief, results and experience that the reader needs.

If you REALLY believe that saving 10% of your earnings will give you a stress-free retirement, you will do it. Your actions may not be easy, but your beliefs will eliminate any debate in your mind.

STEP 3: Results

Seeing tangible results from the action we take instills confidence and MORE BELIEF in a person. Shedding 2 pounds on a weight loss program empowers us to not only believe in the system but ourselves. The results always come at a price that we were unable or unwilling to pay in the past. These new results along with the reinforcement from our coach/trainer are necessary to stimulate more belief and more of the action necessary to complete our goal.

If you have diligently saved 10% of your salary for 10 years, you will have something to show for it. This result is critical to reinforcing your belief that your actions were correct. Conversely, if you squandered your savings, your "belief" of saving 10% is not supported. This disconnect spirals you sideways, down and away from success.

When you generate a thought, support it with knowledge, act on it and get a result from it - it becomes part of your life experience – not just a passing thought that is often forgotten.

Your belief creates your action. Your action creates a result and that reinforces your belief. The circle spirals up and solidifies your process.

A person's belief also affects the people and environment that surrounds them. When my belief is shared with others, people can reject it or embrace it. The entire foundation for religion and theology in the world is based upon this principle of instilling belief in others.

Nothing is more powerful than the ability to influence.

Even thought the belief-action-results (B.A.R.) model is more thorough than any one of its individual parts, application and achievement can still be a temporary victory. There are scores of people who have lost weight and gained it back or achieved success only to have it be a temporary win, instead of a permanent habit or character trait.

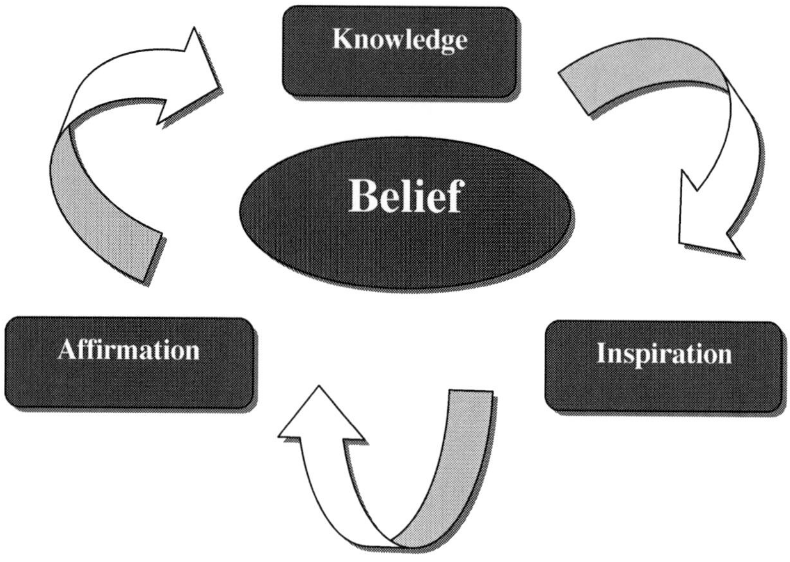

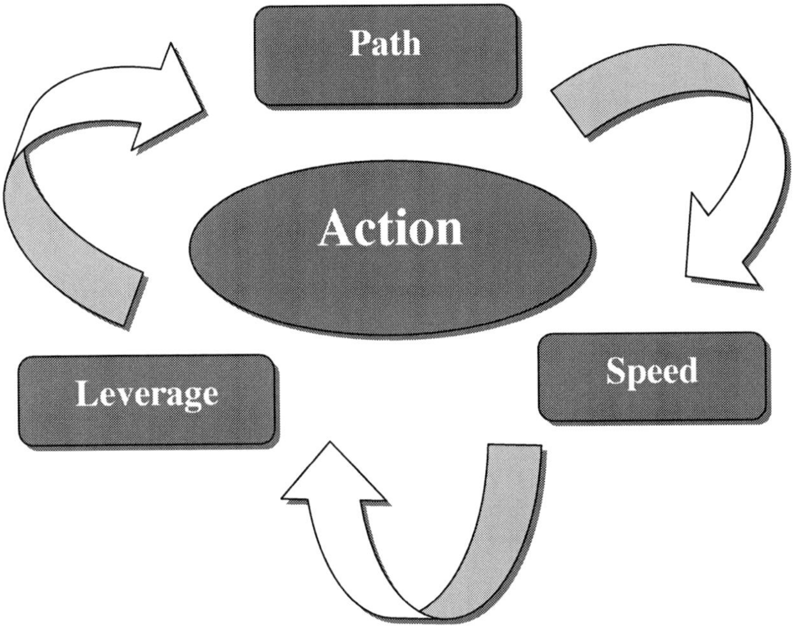
Path
Action
Leverage
Speed

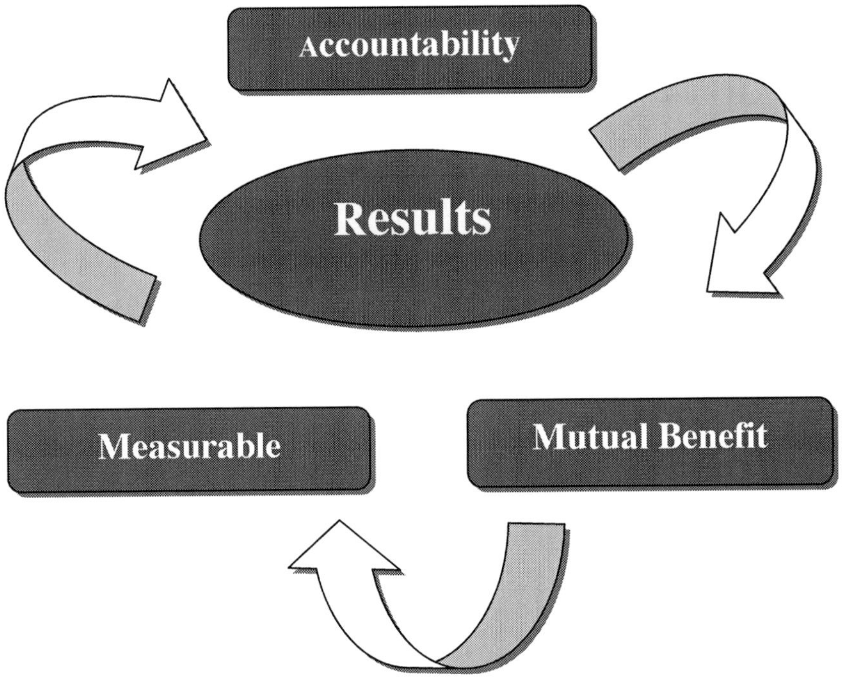
Accountability
Results
Measurable
Mutual Benefit

The B.A.R. system cannot function long term without a synergistic application to the world around us. The only way for a goal to affect the pursuer on a permanent and truly life-changing basis is to spiral the model out to other people and the environment around us. Even a deeply personal goal will affect our environment and the people around us. The 3 dimensional model of BARB is what causes accountability and **PERMANENT** results. In section III, you will apply your new beliefs, action and results to the world around you causing a chain reaction of success. Pretty cool-right?

What you are about do is revolutionary. In fact, it is evolutionary! You're going to read something, you're going to interact with me, the author, and you're going to be accountable with another person who is going to help you apply what you learn in your life and then you're going to help others to do the same.

You aren't going to simply read this book. You are going to have a three-dimensional, experiential event.

This book *will not* deliver if you simply read it. It will give you temporary encouragement, but it won't change your life. Of course I want you to read it. But that is only the beginning. Instilling hope or motivation is easy. But, giving you hope is not the goal. Delivering hope, courage and conviction is part of the process on the path TO that goal. Your goal is to get what YOU want. Maybe you want some or all of the following:

- Lose those last 20 pounds
- Maintain a healthy weight
- Earn an extra $20,000, $50,000 or more a year
- Build a new business that makes you financially free
- Kick the smoking habit once and for all
- Create a happy and loving relationship
- Feel better emotionally
- Eat nutritionally healthy meals-forever
- Have more energy, vitality and awareness
- Become successful and empowered
- Manage your time better

It's a big order – it's an extremely tall order. This is why most of us spend a lifetime running towards it. This is also why only the top 1% of us achieves it. It is easier to watch success than to become successful. Most of us opt to watch the game versus being on the field.

You Have a Team

No man is an island. That's why this breakthrough system allows you to take your situation and goals and create a customized accountability system for yourself. And we're not talking about – with all due respect – an AA meeting where we're around other people with similar problems. Those groups might be helpful and supportive. When dealing with an addiction, that system has proven effective.

When you seek achievement and success, you need somebody who's already achieved the success you desire – period! Enroll in the interactive portion of this book and associate with success. Don't make the mistake made by millions year after year.

If you want to shed extra weight, you don't ask an unhealthy person how to do it. You don't go to a stockbroker who's broke, and you don't go to an athlete who came in 4th place and ask him how to run the race.

You go to the #1 successful person you can find. You are going to network with the best.

"But Doug, I've failed repeatedly time and time again. I read, plan and hope for improvement, but nothing is working lately." My past doesn't have a very good track record. You are not alone. Your mission is to do the following:

Accept your past. Learn from it. Create learning experiences from tragedy. Understand the power of your subconscious mind. Re-wire yourself for successful thoughts, actions and results.

Take the required action consistently and passionately.

Give what you need the most; encouragement, belief & accountability.

Time is so precious. Throughout this book there are references to time, time management and selecting good information. You cannot get time back. All you can do is live in the moment, live in the present and plan the future.

After you finish this book, no longer will you look back and say, "I should have done X." That kind of nonsense is only applicable if you have invented a time machine. You will use your past successes and failures to reflect and LEARN from your past so that you can channel the skills of your wins to doing it again. In other words, if you have been successful in one area, you will apply that same set of skills to other areas of your life.

Regarding your failures, we will painfully examine your thoughts, beliefs and actions that created that failure and not do it again.

You will be allocated a small amount of time to understand why you made a past decision, how they affected you, how you can learn from it.

Your Resources

You may be reading this and think you are starting at zero. In fact, there have been times in my own life where I started at LESS than zero! Regardless of your main objective of increased health, wealth or relationships, you have assets at your disposal. As long as you have air in your lungs and a mind to work out a path, you have what it takes to achieve whatever you want.

Isn't that what we tell children?

In fact, your current set of skills and experiences can be used in other areas of your life. Skill set transfer will be a key component in creating the successes in your life into the areas which you have failed in the past. Now I've heard some people say, "Oh no! I've had a rough life – nothing's gone right for me."

My response is everyone has succeeded at something. The very fact that you are alive and reading this book and are literate is an achievement. You may be failing in the battle with your weight, finances or relationship; but you HAVE succeeded at a previous job, relationship, business, or activity. With a little prodding or with the help of a loved one, you will pull from your past a handful of things that you enjoy, are good at, or have accomplished.

You may have been 50 pounds overweight your entire life but you've been successful at something else. It might have been your family, it might have been your career, and it might have been doing something for another human being in motivating them or being supporting a family member or friend. It could've been anything. Whatever it was we're going to dig that out of you and you're going to help someone else in that area where they need your help. You are unique.

Who Are You

By understanding the basics of personality you will interact better with others, especially yourself. Moreover, your enrollment in the Bexsi[tm] system will give you a printed action plan, delivered electronically in minutes from completing your interaction. Premium members get a hardbound edition along with our exclusive Nag-O-Matic[tm] system.

Everybody as a unique personality and qualities that make them unique all personalities are broken up into four quadrants. We all have a combination of all 4 personalities, but we also have a dominant personality. Read the following four titles, mantras and descriptions. Which one best describes you?

Actors: The Life of the Party

Mantra: "Fire, ready…who needs to aim?"

Actors are people with strong social skills. They are very good at winning over their friends, strangers, even enemies. They enjoy being in the lime light.

An Actor will always be eager to please others especially if they are given attention for their outgoing, friendly ways. They also enjoy the recognition from other people and generally get involve with things that come easily to them. Nothing motivates an Actor like a quick fix and a public affirmation. Instant thrills and fast-paced action motivates them.

When Actors interact with people, they sell themselves to others and even try to win their point of view if it differs. Often, in spite of their outgoing and winning personality, other personalities perceive them as show-offs and manipulative.

Most of the time, they tend to disregard the feelings of others. They do not know they have offended someone even though they thought it was a really funny joke (normally to gain the attention of others at the expense of the poor friend). Amusing themselves is a full-time endeavor.

An Actor may also appear to others an attention seeking, liar. While an Actor's perception of him or herself is that of a professional story-teller. Exaggerating an event to make a point is their mode of communication.

They are people who respect strength and will often trample over weaker people. If you are an n Actor, you will be:

- A person who uses openness to build trust

- Loves applause, sincere feedback and being the center of attention
- A person who embraces excitement and risks
- Tends to save cut corners to save time
- Likes to gain visibility and exposure in the eyes of others
- Will be influenced by anything that appeals to them emotionally
- Is probably disorganized and may appear scatter-brained
- Will be the life of the party; the center of attention
- Is charismatic and charming
- Often shares qualities of a Director

Directors: Control Freak

Mantra: "Aim, fire, ready"

Directors are perceived as active, independent, confident and results oriented. He or she may appear to be bossy at times or even disregard other people's feelings when it comes to getting things done.

They are very forceful and strong willed and may tend to take charge of everything especially when they see a colleague, project partner or subordinate doing something wrong or slowly.

They usually appear rushed and will do anything to save time in the name of efficiency. Directors also have very high standards and will be seen as very competent in getting the job done but may push people too hard and sometimes even wondering why those people don't respond to orders or move too slowly.

Directors also tend to lack patience when dealing with others. They don't like repeating instructions and solving the same problem over and over again.

A director's need for personal success will also become counter-productive as they limit their ability to work as a team with others because they will hoard the entire task to themselves. If you are a director, your will be:

- Obsessed with efficiency and saving time
- Enjoys beating your opposition to the ground
- Measure the value of everything in results
- Gets along well with people who will comply with you
- Can appear overbearing and controlling
- Are natural leaders
- Likes to find out what is the solution to getting things done
- Does things that gain immediate result
- Thrives best when given the freedom to make all the decisions
- May share some qualities of an Actor

Writer: Laid Back and Witty

Mantra: "Ready, aim, fire."

Writers are very good friends. They are very casual and likable people that would go all out to please others. They are the peace makers. They tend to minimize conflict with other people.

When it comes to making decisions, they generally let others make the decisions and will rarely turn down the request. They may sometimes be perceived by others as having no back-bone because of their complying attitude and lack of initiative.

They are also people who do not respond well to challenges and are not usually highly-competitive people. This is because they do not want to hurt the feelings of others when winning or losing in a competitive environment and may even 'let others win' to preserve the friendship.

They are people who respond well to orders (especially from Directors). This makes them very easy to supervise but not when it comes to having them do things on their own without supervision. They also tend to lack interest in planning and goal-setting and may need to be more ordered when it comes to doing things.

There is no point asking them for honest or critical advice because they then to sugar coat the feedback in an effort not to hurt anyone.

When a Writer faces disagreement, they tend to let others have their way while building a wall of resentment in themselves until they finally explode (and then apologizing profusely afterwards). If you are a writer, you will be:

- Leaning towards projects that promise rewards and more friends
- Will do anything to save a relationship
- Enjoys people that provide companionship and mutual cooperation
- Views attention from friends and loved-ones an utmost priority
- Lacking urgency in doing things
- Poor time management
- Builds trust through acceptance
- Shares qualities of a Producer

Producers: Obsessive Compulsive

Mantra: "Ready, aim…aim some more."

A producer is a type of person who uses a methodical problem solving method approach to life. They tend to lean more towards good ideas, complex concepts and intriguing solutions rather than towards feelings. They also like study and analysis of the topics they are interested in.

When it comes to making decisions however, their knowledge does not help them; rather it hinders them from making timely decisions. The term – *Paralysis of Analysis* tends to describe them best. They tend to procrastinate too much until they 'find the best solution'.

Normally when you put to similar producers together, they can entertain each other for hours dissecting, hair-splitting ideas and spend the whole day discussing theories and situations and all kinds of things relating to their topic of interest. On the other hand, when it comes to talking to others, they tend to bore others and they wonder why nobody will listen to their great ideas and analysis!

Producers are the most well organized people in the world and perhaps the only group who enjoy doing the dishes. Their charts, graphs, statistics, schedules, calendars and diaries are probably the most beautiful pieces of artwork they own.

Producers thrive in situations where they are in an advisory role and relate well to others through information. However, they don't respond well to pressure and will be rendered ineffective when it comes to high-pressure situations. If you are a Producer, you will be:

- The king of knowledge and will thrive in situations where information is needed
- Measures progress by the number of activities
- Has an overly detailed time management style
- Builds trust with others through reliability
- Always asks the question HOW because it relates to technical things
- Will do anything that ensures safety and gains certainty
- Is influenced to decide through detailed plans and well charted arrangements

- Shares qualities of a Writer

Nobody is 100% any of these personalities, of course. Everyone has qualities of all four. However, most people have a dominant personality.

Are you a Producer? Do you enjoy numbers? Are you methodical? Do you analyze things again and again? If I were to come over to your house and look in your dresser drawer, would you socks be organized?

How about the Actor personality? Are you the life of the party? Do you lose your car keys frequently? Do you lose your car? Do you like adventure and surprises?

Perhaps you are a Director. Do you get more done than most? Do you have a high drive to succeed? Are you the type that shoots first and ask questions later?

Or maybe you are a Writer. Writers have a dry wit. Many are musically inclined. If you are a Writer, you are a good facilitator and you rarely rock the boat.

Register for the online version of this book and you can take our brief personality quiz and you'll know exactly what your dominant and secondary personality is.

How does your personality relate to these two areas of your life, your failures and your success? If you are a director personality you've beaten yourself up, got back up on the horse and went at it again.

If you're a producer personality you probably analyzed your failures made specific steps to correct them and moved along.

If you are a writer personality you're probably reflecting on it, thinking about it and might never ever get over it.

If you are an actor personality you probably didn't even know you made a mistake and if you did you laughed it off and just moved on and tried something different with absolutely no plan to back it up.

A Complete Solution

This is not just a book.

Your journey to become healthier, wealthier or wiser is not simply motivating you to take action. This book is the first step in a revolutionary accountability system to take you wherever you want to go!

Do you want to stick with your pain management program? Are you interested in doubling your sales and need to be more effective?

Would you like to get to a healthy weight and STAY there? Is kicking the smoking habit difficult?

Would increasing your grades by a full point or two make your life better?

Regardless of your goal or objective, this system can finally get you there. We are going to do this with a COMPLETE approach to change. This time you are going to not only make better choices and stick to the goal, but you are about to involve yourself with an accountability system that will not allow you to deviate, pause or quit. You are in the race for your very life and it is time to make it happen. The metaphor of Express Lane to Success is important. You are in a race for a better life. Only THIS time, you have a race car, full of gas, a better roadmap, mechanic and maintenance. This time you will win.

When you apply the breakthrough system outlined in this interactive book, you can create permanent, positive change in your life that will skyrocket you to your ideal self. Am I going to motivate you there? Certainly motivating ourselves by reading rags to riches stories of others all by itself isn't working. If the secret to permanent, positive improvement was to be inspired for a few hours, simply watching the Olympics would get you off your rear and into the gym.

• • •

"Insanity is doing the same thing over and over again, while expecting a different result."

~ Anonymous

• • •

What Is Required

Below are the 3 requirements for using this book, achieving the RESULTS that you want and eliminating the option for failure. They are simple and your only requirements are to decide right now on the following three things:

#1. Finish This Book. You have to go through it in its entirety. You can't skip chapters. You can't say "I will read but not go online" you have got to go through the entire system.

#2. No Opt Out. You are not going to opt out. Once you are finished with the book and have engaged the accountability system you are in. You're not allowed to quit. It's not an option. If you're going to do that return the book and I'll send you your money back.

#3. Use Everything. Help somebody else out during your transformative process. Richard David Bach once wrote, "You teach best what you most need to learn." So engage the entire system at www.bexsi.com and be an accountability partner for someone else.

By paying it forward, by being a giver, we're going to selfperpetuate this entire system. Not just for you but for the world. If you are going to change your beliefs, take the necessary action and finally get the permanent results you want, you may as well do it right. Become involved 100%. Give.

Ready to get started? Let's go.

Your Struggles - "Bring 'em on!"

Imagine a story where the child grows up in a perfect household, has the perfect education, is in perfect health, has a sphere of influence of people that they could call on and talk with and reflect to and learn from, has an extremely high IQ, is perfectly prepared for school, for college, for his career, has achieved wisdom beyond intelligence and has been able to harness their mind and achieve great things, they've been able to influence others and have unlimited capital resources.

Some of you would call it a fairy tale. Most of us would hate that kid! There's nothing to it. It's not inspirational – it's not even fun to listen to. We much prefer to hear a story where the kid was poor, abused, handicapped and had the IQ of a turnip before winning the Pulitzer Prize. Of course when we read THOSE stories, some might say, "He was lucky!"

Make up your mind! If the silver spoon boy is lucky, then you would believe that all success is based on luck. If you vote for the 2nd kid, you probably don't want to say he was "lucky" to have all those misfortunes, but you might say that those misfortunes shaped him and made him stronger.

Take luck out of the equation.

If you believe that luck is any part of the equation of success, then any excuse will work. Why not simply give up now. Just return this book and go back to the end of the line. Luck is nothing more than being in the right place at the right time and you can't put yourself in the path of luck by simply thinking about being in those paths– you have to get off your butt, walk out the door and do it.

And that's what this book and system is all about: You are going to place yourself in the path of your own success.

Put another way, your life's journey has infinite possibilities. There are limitless roads you can take towards your goal. Many of these highways will lead you to what you want and deserve. Many more are dead ends or will circle you back to square one. We are going to put gas in your tank, put an accountability partner in the seat next to you, get out a roadmap that will clearly mark the best route to take, and put you on the express lane to success. This express lane is in existence today. Your only job is to put yourself in the seat, buckle up, read the instructions and put your foot on the gas. Let's go.

So far there's been one huge obstacle to your success and you know what it is – It's NOT your health, it's not your finances, it's not the environment, it's not your circumstances, it's not your spouse, it's not your kids, it's not your boss, and it's not the economy.

The single largest obstacle to your success – You got it – it's YOU!

• • •

I went to a bookstore and asked the saleswoman, "Where's the self-help section?" She said if she told me, it would defeat the purpose.

~George Carlin

• • •

Here's proof. You're not around your boss all day. You're not around your kids all day. You're not interacting with the environment or the economy all day. But you are around one thing all day long, 24/7, your entire life;

You are constantly in touch with your thoughts, belief and actions.

The only thing to fix – the only thing you really need to work on – the only thing we CAN work on – the only thing you have 100% power over, is you. Sure, we'll give you some new perspectives on the motivation you need to win this time. I will pepper the lessons with real life stories of inspiration, hope and redemption. But if you simply read this book and think that things will get better because of your positive attitude, you are going to fail…again.

Making the Decision to Change

How do you begin on your Express Lane to Success? January 1st is littered with the thing called New Year's resolutions. I am guilty as perhaps you are, with setting New Year's resolutions and quitting New Year's resolutions generally within 20 days. That's generally the time the health clubs fill up. On January 1st and 2nd they overbook membership by about 40 to 50 percent. But by January 20th they are back to normal levels – the committed group of people, those with personal trainers that have paid for a full year in advance, have already made their commitments. They have acted and they have committed to their plan of attack to be healthier.

So, if you want more wealth, health and happiness in your life you need to start with a thought followed by an action. Your first choice of words may not be the right one. At first, many words come to mind such as commitment, action and motivation. There are defeatist words that also crop up like trying, resetting and trying again. Only the RIGHT ones will be drilled into your belief system, and none of those words are important yet.

The first and only word to understand before you change your attitude, habits and life is the word, DECISION. You need to *decide* to act. You can't act until you have decided to do so.

Deciding is step one. What are you deciding to do? There are a number of thoughts, feelings and physical actions you must decide to do. However, understanding the decision process is critical for the following reasons:

You need to make the RIGHT decision.

You need to not back out of your decisions.

Your decision must be supported by your thoughts, feelings, and reinforcement tools on a constant basis.

Without understanding your decision making process you will be doomed to making a weak decision, backing out of them too early, or justifying your new decisions. None of these decision-making processes work.

Perhaps in the past you "decided" to begin exercising every day. The first day was tough, but you were motivated. The second day your muscles were sore, but you persisted. Since you pushed through those first few days, you felt justified in taking the next day off. You know the rest of the story.

By giving yourself an option to change your decision, you've not only made the wrong choice but the "other voice" in your head justified it and the internal excuses started flowing.

By the same token, making a decision based on false information does you no good. How many times have you been told to diversify your portfolio? "Never put your eggs all in one basket," this age old advice states. That kind of "one size fits all" advice isn't backed up by the facts. According to the book, "The Millionaire Next Door" 70% of all millionaires own their own businesses and put ALL their eggs into one basket. (The remaining 30% do the same; they're called doctors, lawyers and other high paid professionals who invest years of their life to a single basket of eggs) Millionaires never diversify on their *journey* to millionaire status. Their diversification only begins once they have a substantial enough portfolio to diversify with. Making the right decision requires getting the correct information from a trusted source, not a marketing brochure.

Decide to act.

Act properly and don't deviate. Your decision to become an unwavering force of nature will insure your path to victory more than any other component of your success. While it will be important and imperative that you ingrain the right attitude and act congruently with the principles of success, nothing can replace your decision to actually DECIDE!

Have you decided to decide? I know it sounds goofy but do it anyway. Waffling on your future decisions will waste your time and consequently you will waste important chunks of your LIFE! You have in your hands all the tools and motivation necessary to create the permanent change you want. But before we barrel ahead, full force towards attaining your dreams, it is important to understand what happened last year! (Or the last few years as you failed to achieve what you thought you could)

If you don't take a cold, hard and honest look back upon your failures, you will repeat them.

Learn from the Past

Look back. Don't beat yourself up, but look back upon what you believed, what you did and what you were thinking. This is the first and last time we are going to look to your past. Think about the events from your past, good and bad and consider the following questions:

What happened?
(Example: I started a new business and after 6 months, I burned through $12,000 and dissolved the business.)

What were you positive thoughts about it?
(Example: All the marketing materials looked positive. I liked the representation.)

How did you validate this information?
(Example: I called a few references)

When you reflect honestly about your failures, do you blame?

The economy? Millions are made in good times or bad. That excuse doesn't work.

Your parents? There are as many success stories from orphans as there are from kids from intact homes.

Your metabolism?
You'll find encyclopedia sized books from people who have cured themselves of overeating, obesity and an unhealthy lifestyle.

Your senator? This one might actually be true.

The bottom line is that for every example of blame or excuse you can find an equal (and frankly a more inspiring story) of success despite the odds. Excuses are created by losers. Only the winners are allowed to tell their story. The tragic story of a person who dies with their potential inside them is too common to be of any interest.

Are you ready right now to eliminate excuses from your vocabulary?

Prove it.

Go online, right now and register for your FREE trial of our accountability system at www.bexsi.com.

Chapter Two

• • •

"If a movie can cause a tear in your eye, you have the power to control your subconscious mind to create miracles."

~Doug Crowe

• • •

You Are Schizophrenic

There are two different types of thought processes that we need to understand and control. You have a subconscious mind and a conscious mind. The more you understand and harness these two aspects of your mind, the more power you wield over your future.

Your subconscious mind is the miracle worker. This is the one that works tirelessly at 100% capacity, 24/7 for the rest of your life. Being able to tap into this and channel its power and throttle it up like a high-powered engine can empower you beyond your comprehension.

We know that there is a tremendous difference in function between the conscious and the subconscious mind. Your conscious mind is analytical, decisive and requires more time to soak in information, process it and spit out an answer. The conscious mind is the only part of the human brain that technically "thinks." Your conscious mind takes in information, makes a decision to act, and then direct the appropriate muscles to act. In addition to processing instant information, the conscious mind will take information from previous experiences to determine the relevancy to the information it is absorbing in the present. Once the past and present is all dumped into your bucket of consciousness, and the options are weighed, a decision is made (even NOT making a decision is a decision!) and the body then acts in accordance with that decision. Whew!

The conscious mind accepts or rejects incoming information on a constant basis.

Here is the fun part.

Your mind is capable of only holding onto one thought at a time. It is possible to bounce between two thoughts, but your brain cannot hold onto two opposing thoughts simultaneously.

What is even more amazing is the interaction between the conscious and subconscious mind. Whenever the conscious mind says "yes" to a piece of incoming information, the subconscious instantly accepts it and reacts without question or delay. Here's an example:

Let's say you are walking between two large panel trucks parked on the side of a street. As you walk out onto the street, you hear the blaring sound of horn, the screech of braking tires and you instantly swing your head to look to the left and see an oncoming car.

The series of thoughts and decisions take less than a second in real time but a few paragraphs to explain. Just pretend it is happening in slow motion.

Your conscious mind compares that oncoming automobile with all other moving automobiles to determine whether or not the automobile is relevant to your safety. If the automobile is a block away then it is not relevant to your immediate safety. Your decision may be to turn your head so you don't see that little lost puppy getting creamed by the car.

If the automobile is much closer and speeding out of control towards you, that would cause a different set of decisions in your brain. You may quickly attempt to judge the swerves to avoid getting hit; you may freeze in panic and utter a certain word that sounds like "sit."

The instance that the conscious mind decides that you should take action and run in a certain direction, your subconscious operator of your nervous system says "get me out of here." Your primal need to survive overrides any need for a discussion by your conscious mind. The entire subconscious operates the autonomic nervous system and all the muscles and nerves and instantly we jump back out of the way of the car.

If your conscious mind was in control of the whole affair, it would have to make choices. The conversation in your conscious mind would be asking questions like, "Should I move my foot to the right or should I finish this sandwich because it is clearly my last meal." Since our subconscious mind is in control at this point we don't go have to go through this exercise and thank goodness for that. Otherwise, humans would not have evolved at all. The subconscious mind tells us to say "yes" to move out of the way of the car the entire body reacts instantaneously.

We use the same reaction not only with situations, but with certain thoughts regarding fear. If we see something or hear something fearful it doesn't matter if it is real or not. The moment we accept that fear as danger, our body reacts with a shot of adrenaline and the "fight or flight" response kicks in automatically. The conscious mind accepts the fear, the subconscious mind accepts it totally and our whole body reacts instantaneously.

Your subconscious mind doesn't make choices. It doesn't have a sense of time. It reacts.

Subconscious Ninja

This incredible tool in our head has been used for millions of years for survival. Since your subconscious takes information at face value, it is easy to fool. Since it has no sense of time, you can use it like a time machine to create a new reality for yourself. Like a samurai warrior, you are going to exploit this weakness and use it for our advantage.

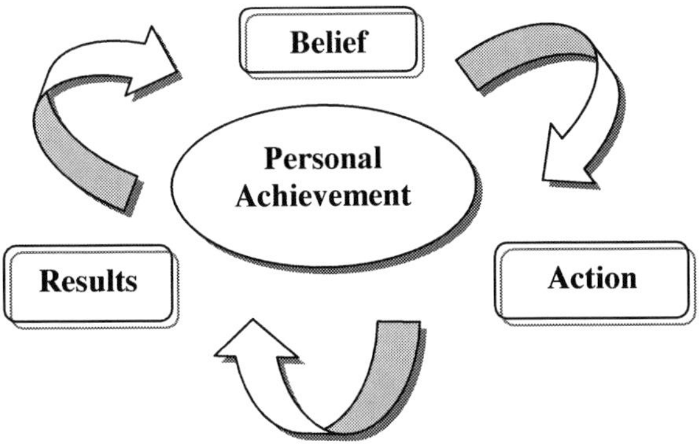

Harnessing your subconscious mind is one of the most powerful tools in your toolbox. By using well constructed affirmations, you can direct the subconscious mind to act instantly to your situation.

It is the process where belief creates action, action creates a result and the result reinforces your belief.

When your actions become habit, your habits will create your lifestyle. "Breaking" a habit is tough. For many people it is nearly impossible. Re-wiring your thoughts, actions and beliefs can replace a habit, which is different than breaking one. That is the reason the character "Kojak" played by Telly Savalas sucked on a lollipop...he had replaced his smoking habit for suckers, thereby trading lung cancer for periodontal disease. Seems like a reasonable trade off.

In section II, you are going to start writing down and verbalizing affirmations. Every time you write an affirmation down, what it is, what you're willing to do for it, and who's going to benefit from it, you'll write it down in the present tense. "I *earn* $100,000 a year. I *have given* an extra 20 hours a week of work to earn it. My family *has taken* nice vacations and *takes care* of my retirement because of it." You write those down and speak them into existence. You're going to read your affirmations in your own voice. By listening to your own voice your conscious action will begin to program your subconscious mind that this is the reality of your life. Recording these affirmations and hearing them via your Bexsi voicemail will be a little uncomfortable at first. Surely you don't mind trading temporary discomfort for a lifestyle of abundance-do you?

Don't skip ahead to section II just yet. You will have the rest of your life for creating, reinforcing and directing your subconscious mind. Before you do that, you need to understand the other voices in your head!

The last time you had to decide whether to hit the snooze alarm or go to the gym, you had one voice saying, "10 more minutes" and the other saying, "Get up lazy butt!"

Devil and Angel on Your Shoulder

The two voices in your head are in constant conflict. The devil on your shoulder is often disguised as the angel (and vice versa). It is up to you to calmly and honestly tell yourself which one has the RIGHT information and words to pull you closer to your goal.

These two sneaky voices have names. We will call one of them your negative self (NS) and the other one will be called your positive self (PS).

Will it make a difference if you hit that snooze button? "10 minutes won't make a difference" NS tells your body. "10 minutes every day over the course of this year equals over 60 hours of time or a FULL WEEK of working time. What could you do with an extra WEEK every year?" says PS. "But those extra 10 minutes feel SO Good and waking up slowly is better for my body," states your NS or is that you PS?

You see? The justification and excuses cloud your judgment. NS is so powerful and so good at justification. That voice is more devious than a master CIA spy. It is up to you to build up defenses against the excuses, empower the right habits in your life in order to hone the skills of success and spread them in all areas of your life.

Your Tragic Past

The difference between tragedy and humor is time. When you have an event such as slipping on a banana peel and the person falls or hurts themselves it's a tragedy, it's painful, it hurts. But if that person falls on a banana peel, gets up, walks down the street for another 30 seconds and then shouts out in pain that creates humor. Put in another way, a story of personal tragedy – an embarrassing moment, a fumbled football, or a misstep at a dance can be "tragic" when it occurs, but becomes humorous over the years. These are embarrassing to the person and may cause them to sweat, to be embarrassed and to turn red during their mild failure. When you tell that story a year or two later it's humorous.

Time plus tragedy equals humor.

Let's apply that principle to the learning process and your perception of the events of your life. Use any example from your own life; the time you were fired from a job, the time you lost $20,000 in the stock market, or the time you got divorced. Think about that tragic event right now.

When you look at that tragedy you may relive it in your brain and have bad feelings, anger or depression. Those events, like a wake from a boat are behind you. Yet your mind, subconscious and conscious are pulling the thoughts of it and regurgitating the negative feelings of the past. It doesn't matter what it is because your subconscious mind has no concept of time.

What that presents to you is a wonderful opportunity.

Regardless of the event, you can reframe that event and create a positive feeling from it right now. This takes some doing depending on the event, so you may not want to pick a real doozy. Let's pass on the death of a loved one for now-OK? Choose a small or medium sized event that brought you down, created depression, rejection or disappointment. Write down the following bits of information:

Write down exactly what happened.
What was the negative effect on your life?
How long ago did it occur?
Who else was affected?
What did you learn from it?
How did you apply what you learned?

In the case of a divorce, perhaps you learned how to communicate better with your new partner. From that experience, perhaps you became a better parent, son or daughter.

Maybe you lost a job because of something you did or didn't do. What did you do DIFFERENTLY on your next job so as not to repeat that mistake? Did you get a better job? Did you start a new career?

Regardless of the event, search deep into your life experience and write down 3 or more things that you learned and how you applied what you learned. If you can't do that, by the end of this book, you will be able to.

You need to reframe that event no matter how tragic it was. If you don't create a framework to learn from it, the event will remain a tragedy and a painful memory creating a feedback loop of defeat. By finding the humor and/or benefit of that event you have reframed it. With this reframing technique you not only create better feelings about the event, you trained your mind to do it again for the future. This unleashes incredible creativity and positive energy into your life and the lives of those around you.

• • •

"Reject your sense of injury and the injury itself will disappear."

~Marcus Aurelius
Roman Emperor

• • •

The Odds Were Not In His Favor

A young boy was born into the world, like thousands of others that day. It was a typical September day in the United States of America. The year was 1971. Two years later, the father leaves his family.

Strike one.

The boy's mother later married a wholesale salesman, who adopted him in 1974. This is her third marriage and it too, will end in divorce.

Strike two.

Despite an imbalanced home life, the boy enjoyed sports. An accomplished athlete, the boy's future looked bright and it seemed nothing could stop him.

At the peak of his sports career he was diagnosed with cancer. He had stage 3 testicular cancer that had already spread to his lymph nodes and brain. Even with treatment his future looked bleak. Doctors told the athlete that he had a 50-50 chance of survival – he actually only had about a 3% chance but doctors wanted him to keep his spirits up.

For the average person, this would have been strike three.

He had the surgery, radiation therapy and had one of his testicles removed. Miraculously he beat the odds and survived cancer. He was declared cancer-free the next year and was able to make a full recovery. He was even able to not only take up sport again but able to compete in and win the Tour de France 7 times in a row. Lance Armstrong is more than an inspiration; he is the poster child for success.

Simply because you beat cancer in your testicles, lymph nodes and brain THEN went on to win the Tour De France seven years in a row, doesn't mean that you are immune from future tragedy, however!

Participating in the Tour De France occurs over a matter of a few weeks. During the rest of the year, life can keep putting up obstacles, challenges and roads that lead to nowhere. Lance had to continually battle accusations of drug abuse for years. His personal life was no less stressful with a marriage, divorce and fathering a child out of wedlock.

Acknowledging bad things is the first step. Reframing them to your benefit is difficult at first, but it is the only path to success. Had Lance accepted the cancer, his mind would have acknowledged defeat and even if he survived, he may not have competed again.

Like failure, success isn't permanent. Being the best cyclist in the world doesn't mean your personal life is a bed of roses. It is never too soon stop resting on your laurels of success. Just as there are terrific stories of struggles and success, there are an equal amount of stories of people who have had it all and lost it.

Financial success, becoming a celebrity or attaining an ideal weight does not guarantee a permanent continuation of that achievement. For that reason alone, your initial focus will be on improving your fundamentals before taking strategic action towards a specific goal, task or objective.

Take the first step *right now*.

Think about your most recent painful experience and write down exactly what you learned from it. The good news is you don't even need a near death experience like testicular/brain cancer as a wakeup call.

Any tragedy will do.

Skill Set Transfer

What about your successes? One magical tool of the Express Lane to Success is going to be sharing your success with another person. It doesn't matter if you've been beat up, abandoned, handicapped or miserable.

You are unique.

You are special.

This isn't just talk. This isn't "feel good" hype. Scientifically, you are the most complex organism in the universe. With over 60,000 miles of blood vessels and 100,000,000,000 neurons your body alone is a miracle like no other. Not only are you a miracle of complexity but you have the potential unlike no other creature on the planet. Even if you are uneducated, handicapped and broke your brain and body have more potential than all the other creatures on the planet combined.

You are amazing.

Because you have the potential for greatness doesn't mean, however, that you have been tapping into it. Urban legend and crackpot science has touted the fact that we use only 10% or 30% of our brain. The evidence is inconclusive on this subject.

Ask any person who has built a business, raised a disabled child or ran a marathon and they will all tell you that you always have untapped potential both mental and physical at your disposal.

Your next exercise is to recall and write down the one thing in you past, that you are proud of. No matter who you are, you have a passion, talent or achievement that is not only unique to you, but you are proud of. When you manifested that accomplishment you did it with a certain set of skills, attitudes or ideals.

Transferring the feeling of success to yourself and your failures is going to be the magic fuel propels you along your Express Lane to Success. Without that experience, without that feeling, and knowledge this will be just another book and your life experience of trial and error will probably repeat itself. Doing the same thing over and over again and expecting a better result - that's ridiculous.

You have had success in the past. Even if you are overweight, broke, divorced, sad, depressed, there was a period in your past where you did something right. Maybe it was five years ago or 20 years ago. Think hard and write it down. You will probably come up with dozens of them. You scored an A on a term paper, you helped an old lady across the street, or you were a successful as a dental technician; you did something that you are proud of.

Whatever it was, YOU did it. Your attitude, skills, experience and belief gave you some type of success. No matter how immaterial it may seem now, it gave you confidence. That confidence you create inside yourself can be used for any endeavor. Incredibly, it can be used for EVERY endeavor.

• • •

"Failure is no more fatal than success is permanent."

~Doug Crowe

• • •

Confidence actually creates tangible power. The only energy required to fuel that power is thought. Your thoughts are the direct and unmistakable conduit to success. Your confidence and skills gave you success, and you buried it. Your job is to share it with others. It's time to use that power to help yourself and others.

So, go ahead and clearly write down exactly the one success you had in your life.

What was the success?
What it meant to you?
How was it affirmed by others?

Was your success affirmed by others? When you got the grades, did you get applause, did someone say, "Good job" or "I'm impressed"? The affirmation of the success of your past is critical for your future. Affirming your self-esteem will reprogram you for success in any area.

Most people who fail repeatedly spend a lot of time and lot of energy reminding themselves of their failure. "Oh gosh I screwed up". Reliving the screw up is useful only one time-when you have learned to NOT do it again!

However, many people unable to let it go. Anybody who has watched the Winter Olympics has seen a world-class figure skater slip and fall. Now for the previous 30 months during practice they might have fallen quite a bit. In practice, they simply get back up, refine their habits and continue their routine.

During a competition, however, they are pumped and at their best. They rarely make a big mistake. If they do make a minor mistake, they generally keep their pace and performance energy remains at its peak. But as soon as they make a big mistake and actually fall on their keister, what happens next?

They fall again.

You can see it in their eyes as they are visibly shaken. Their performance is doomed and they know it. They've lost not only physically, but mentally as well.

The psychological reason for this "spiral down" is not simply because they are embarrassed by their mistake. What happens is that in their minds' eye while they are continuing on in their performance and skating their hearts out physically, at a subconscious level they are reliving that mistake. And that error continuously crops up in their head and is transferred into their body.

The same thing is true on performances that go well. When a team plays on their home court they are said to have the "home field advantage." Home field advantage means you have more fans and the audience cheering you on so there are more people saying "Hey you can do this...You are our team."

Statistically, the home field advantage is an undeniable fact. That audible reinforcement of your success of your self esteem is not just for somebody who is broken, busted and disgusted; it applies to professional multimillionaire athletes. So, self-esteem programming is a critical step and has to be done on a continuous basis.

Transferring your skills can be done with any skill you have.

It is up to you to categorize them, write them down and remind your conscious mind of your past achievements. Your subconscious mind will pick it up as if it was yesterday. Remember, your subconscious mind has no sense of time.

You may be a poor athlete, but a great student. Use it.

Perhaps you are terrible at writing, but a good speaker. Hire out someone to support your weaknesses and focus on your strengths.

Maybe you are great at being organized at work, but your home is a mess. Treat your home as a part-time business. Get your family to become your staff. You don't need to pay them a salary, but you can engage their assistance in creating a more organized home if they all treat it with as much respect as you treat your job.

You may have great habits at work. You show up on time, you leave late and always get great reviews. However, you can't seem to develop the habit of reducing your caloric intake and exercising on a daily basis. Again, by transferring the skills you have at work to your personal or social life, you can become incredibly effective.

All you have to do is remind yourself of your success and treat your weakness with the same skills as your success. You can do it.

Forgive Yourself

After you put in writing the reframing of your negative experience, you should also take responsibility for the results. Since you are not going to pass the buck and blame the economy or your parents, you will look in the mirror and say, "Yup...that was my responsibility." Only after you do that sincerely can you change your thoughts, feelings, beliefs and outcomes through a shift in your attitude and actions. Before we go down that road, however, you must forgive.

The word *forgiveness* is a very misunderstood concept. Most people have trouble with forgiveness especially when dealing with a deep wound. Let's forget about yourself for a moment and think about the last time you upset somebody or they upset you and you either asked for or gave forgiveness. The person who **gives** forgiveness is the person who has the power. When you forgive somebody the only thing you are really doing is taking a load of bricks off your own back. You feel bad, you were hurt, and somebody burned you. The moment you dig deeply into your own heart and forgive that person you have relieved the stress and anxiety from yourself. This is an extremely powerful thing to feel and say. Look in the mirror and say to yourself, "You know what? I forgive you."

Now whether that person deserves forgiveness, has earned it or even knows about it is totally irrelevant. The very fact that you've forgiven that person is done solely to help you lead a better life and to move forward instead of always looking back with angst. It is usually harder for people to forgive themselves than it is to forgive others.

• • •

"When you forgive it takes you from the place of the victim to that of a victor."

~ Unknown

• • •

Forgiving yourself is extremely empowering. The quicker and more consistently you can forgive yourself the more power you create to achieve new goals, new dreams and start a new life. Empower yourself by scraping off the emotional dust and self-loathing scum of your past. Your new knowledge and attitude supported by a spirit of forgiveness will give you the strength to succeed where you have failed in the past. You failed - okay great - chalk it up and move on.

Encouragement

When you don't have the right encouragement, it's very difficult to create the right expectations for yourself. When you don't have the right encouragement, it's nearly impossible to have the belief that you're a winner. When you don't have the encouragement, where do you find that attitude that things happen for a reason? How do you truly believe you're going to learn from it? How do you know it's going to benefit you in the long run?

When you don't have the encouragement for that, what are you left with?

You're left with only one thing - your own self-talk.

The Express Lane to Success System is designed to give you encouragement on multiple levels. You will get it from me, yourself and the fellowship of achievers from our FREE social network at www.besxi.org.

Some of you are very much alone right now. You may be reading this, going through this program, and you're 100% alone, there's nobody out there to help or support you.

In fact, it may be worse than that. There may be dozens of people who are dead set against your success. Most of naysayers are not even doing it on purpose. Frequently, our friends of family believe they are helping you. Unfortunately for most people, these people support a failing attitude or allow you to make and justify the excuses you have.

I have had them, too.

When I started to design and write this interactive book I had a person very close to me say, "Don't push so hard. You might get a heart attack. Forget about that deadline. Maybe it's not meant to be. It's okay."

Without a firm accountability for deadlines, most of us procrastinate on everything. I wasn't about to create an accountability book and interactive system and not finish it. No way.

If you can't get encouragement from your spouse, from your best friend, from your mother, from your kids, from your dog, or from the books you are reading, trade in your discouraging influencers for encouraging ones.

O.K....maybe not the spouse.

If your spouse is negative, just compartmentalize that. Go ahead and say, "I love you, honey. Got to go, I'll be right back," and focus on replacing and assaulting those negative impressions, thoughts and sympathetic B.S. with the positive encouragement that you require.

Any negative input from family, friends, or associates should be filtered as if it were poison, because it is. Read new books, get new friends and stop listening to information that drags you down.

Inserting the RIGHT encouragement into your conscious is imperative. Encouragement is a critical component of belief when you're all by yourself. Transferring that encouragement from your conscious into your subconscious is one of your daily tasks. You have a lifetime of negative influences and your life-long mission is to replace them with positive ones. The positive encouragement you seek is as important as the air in your lungs. You may not need encouragement for survival, but you need it to live.

If you don't have positive, encouraging relationships and you don't know where to start, you can start with me. Drop me a line and I will be your first raving fan! Simply go to www.bexsi.com and contact me.

When you register with our FREE network of achievers, you will not only have me as a new positive encouraging force in your life, you will also have a new network of super achievers.

One of the best ways to receive encouragement is to give it.

Chapter **Three**

• • •

"Sometimes you must give yourself what you wish someone else would give to you."

~Dr. Phil McGraw

• • •

Coach or Cheerleader?

When there's somebody working out with a coach standing or a trainer standing next to you shouting in your ear, "Give me ten more," what is the normal result of that? The person does ten more.

So does encouragement work? Only in a HUGE way!

Remember when you saw your first baby take its first steps, you encouraged him. You didn't say, "He'll never walk. Let him crawl around the rest of his life." Of course not, you always encouraged positive behavior. You're an encourager. And guess what? Now it's your turn.

It's your turn to get encouragement and you're going to get it as often as you need it through the Bexsi[tm] system. You're going to get it every single day through an email, a text, a voicemail, and then once a week, through a personal mentor who's going to give you exactly what you need.

You want and need a bit of encouragement to:

- Create an improved belief system
- Reinforce and grow your beliefs
- Hold you accountable to your action steps
- Encourage you when you miss a milestone
- Support you when you drop the ball
- Remind your of the power of your mind
- And…

Create a clearer perspective on who you are, where you are going and how much more fulfilling your life will be when you take the action required. You will have all the encouragement and new beliefs that you need to be successful.

Your expectations will push you beyond your comfort zone. Your belief system will improve. You have to have the right system of beliefs in your head. You have to have a proper attitude. Expecting the best with the positive attitude and a grateful heart will give you the success that you desire.

Of all the things that affect you - outside forces, from job to school, to friends, to family - the number one person that's battling you right now is yourself. Your encouragement is a powerful tool for yourself and others.

Use it.

My Story of Encouragement

As the author of Express Lane to Success, like all entrepreneurs, I have not always been successful. For five years straight, I wrote down, "I'm a millionaire and I'm 30 years old." Writing "Millionaire by 30" when I'm 31, 32, 33, 34, doesn't really make sense because I'm no longer 30! Of course, I re-wrote it with a NEW deadline each and every year after that.

Year 1: Missed my goal.
Year 2: Missed my goal.
Year 3: Missed it, missed it, and missed it.

The year I hit it, that's when I called my dad and let him know the goal that I had set for all of my life had been attained.

I was a millionaire.

The encouragement I got from my parents and from the evidence of my success, encouraged me to buy more property and to repeat my success. Within a few years, I had become a multimillionaire. Wow.

I founded and developed the nation's only semester-based academy for real estate. I had a school. I built a company. I even had a radio show in Chicago. I bought more property. I taught more people. I gave back to the world without expecting anything in return. Teaching people how to change their financial future by investing in real estate was incredibly fulfilling. I was having the time of my life. I became a developer. I purchased a subdivision, a few apartment buildings and converted them to condominiums. I rolled the profits from one into the potential of the next. Things were going good...actually great.

Then it hit.

Bear Stearns collapsed.

The credit markets collapsed.

Real estate prices dropped.

Then they dropped again. As I worked feverishly to patch things up, slash prices, discount deals and create value, the damage had already been done. It was over. My personal fortune was wiped out. Everything was gone.

I lost every dollar I ever earned.

I lost my identity as a man, as a provider, I was in bankruptcy and I lost all the real estate I owned. I lost my house; I lost my savings account, and nearly lost my family. Strange as it sounds now, there were even a few brief moments that suicide was more appealing than the pain I was in. I had unknowingly inflicted pain on others. I was a mess.

I know what it is like to be up. I know what it is like to be down. Being diagnosed clinically depressed for 6 months, I was encouraged to get on some medication. Being a motivational speaker and a successful person previously, you'd think I could just snap out of it and say, "Well, gee, time to read a good book and get back on that horse," and as much as I tried, I was unable to get back on that horse. There were plenty of times where I had a few of those outer body experiences where you look in the mirror and say, "What is your problem? Get up off your ass and get to work."

For nearly a year I was in emotional quicksand. I couldn't break free. I was done.

The CD in Your Head

The reason encouragement and affirmations are so vital was about to become readily apparent. Fortunately for me (And now, for any Bexsi^{tm} members) I had recorded a short 45 minute CD.

I had recorded this CD at the peak of my career. It contained motivation, testimonials and a 30 page goal setting system that was the seed for this full book and comprehensive program you have in your hands.

Imagine what it must feel like to be clinically depressed and watching over 22 years of wealth, success and happiness evaporate. At the peak of this turmoil, I took a 15 hour drive to try and make one sale. A long shot gamble with one client that may earn me $1,000. While it would not have been enough to even make a mortgage payment, it would help to feed my family. This 2 day, 15 hour gamble didn't pay off. No sale.

As I was driving down the road, wallowing in my pity, I knew that I had to come back. I wanted to resurrect the "old Doug" (A name my family and friends coined during this time). I took a dozen motivational CD's with me for that trip. For the past year I had listened to them with skepticism and disgust. I had achieved success and I had lost it. I remember reading stories about millionaires who had gone bust and built it up again. I told myself that may happen. There is a massive difference between reading about it and living it.

It almost killed me-literally.

There's nothing more humbling than listening to your former successful self, talking to the broke loser you are today and thinking, "Who is that guy?" First of all, we all HATE the sound of our own voice. Listening to that voice of confidence, reason and power, however, created a fundamental shift. Listening to "Old Doug" was my fork in the road. Drugs, time, and all the reading in the world didn't do anything to pull me out of my depression. Listening to that CD on during a 15 hour drive, however, caused an infinitesimal shift.

It was not one of those "Aha" moments. The angels didn't sing and I didn't get a flash of inspiration. It was, however, a small seed of hope that took root. Now it was up to me to nurture it.

Affirmations are critical. Without an affirmation going through your head on a continuous basis, you're going to continue to struggle and have challenges and unknowingly attract negative influences in your life. You can have setbacks. You can have collapses. But even allowing a single depressing or doubtful thought in your head can completely crush your spirit. Interestingly, you already have affirmations going through your head on a consistent basis. The only difference is that you are going to direct them like never before.

Expectation of Belief

When we study success, we find there are several different components. Any of these components in and of themselves will not give you the success you're looking for. However, when you combine these three critical components in a circle, you have an unbreakable chain that guarantees your success as long as you apply the circuit breakers in between these steps to continue on the correct circle because the incorrect circle can spiral you away from your goal and down a path that leads you farther away from it.

Components of Success

Thought

Confidence. Expect to win.
Attitude. Create a positive one.
Knowledge. Seek out wisdom.

Action

Decisiveness. Fortune favors the bold.
Consistency. Repetition is the foundation of excellence.
Leadership. Action without interaction is a hollow victory.

Community

Association. Learn from the very best.
Generosity. Give without expecting anything in return.
Perspective. Patience instills confidence of purpose.

By using these three components and the circuit breakers in between to keep you on the correct path, no force, no circumstance, no events, no thoughts, no person, no job, no family member can push you significantly away from your goal. These three components are the bar system: belief, action and results.

Belief holds the other two together. Belief is the cornerstone of the circle. Your past beliefs have given you the actions that you took and delivered to you the results that you got. By shifting your beliefs you shift your actions and create a new and more powerful result. It is THAT result which fuels future action. Viola!

Belief is powerful. It would be easier to blame the reason you're overweight, the reason you have no money, the reason you're tired, the reason you're disgusted, the reason you're depressed on something other than belief.

Wouldn't it be easier to blame the president or the economy? It will be really easy for us to blame our parents – our upbringing, our circumstances, a death, a divorce or anything other than that person in the mirror. A lot of things can affect people but if we take a look at supportive stories of people who have been in worse situations than you and I have ever been in, it takes away those excuses of outside circumstances whether they are health, or money, or extenuating circumstances beyond our control. None of these are to blame for our failures in the past.

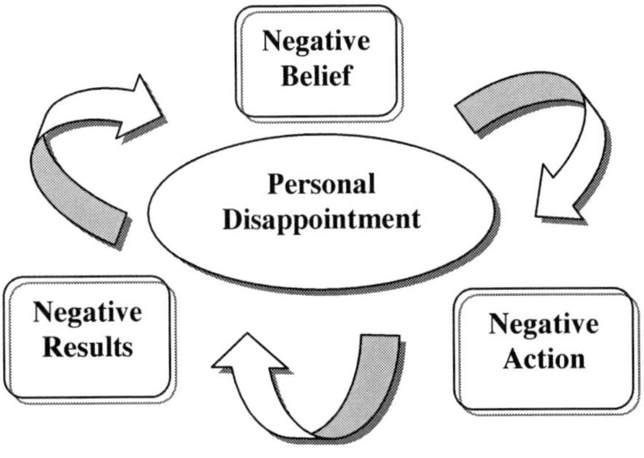

The only thing to look at and not to blame but the only thing to consider and to reorganize and to change and the first thing we have to change is *our beliefs*. You are fat because you believe you're supposed to be that way. You are broke because you believe that's your lot in life and being a millionaire is only for a select few. You are depressed because you think that the world has given you bad luck. It matters to you now because your belief is wrong and that's what we're going to change right now. It may be difficult to change your beliefs when faced with a reality that says otherwise. But, without a shift in your defeating beliefs, you will be doomed to a self-fulfilling prophecy.

The B.A.R. model works for OR against you.

Even the hint of failure gives fuel to the negative expectation of disappointment. Refusing to allow doubt is extremely important.

When you change your belief, you can change your outcomes. Having the proper attitude about a bad event, a dismal failure or a painful circumstance can mold that into a lesson of success. But *a belief is going to change the outcome of your future*.

Your vision is what creates your future. It's the foundation for that action. If I believe that eating a jelly doughnut every single day was going to make me healthy, I would do it all day long. But I don't eat a jelly doughnut everyday because I know it won't give me the health in a week that I want. If I believe that reducing sugars in my diet, daily exercise and eating fewer carbohydrates will make a permanent difference, then I will act accordingly. If I only eat when I'm hungry, and not when I'm sad, depressed or frustrated, then I'll have a healthy lifestyle and I'll have a weight and energy level that can measure up with my age and who I am. But if your belief is messed up and messes up your actions it messes up your results.

If you don't act in concert with your beliefs, you're in a convoluted state.

Your B.A.R. model of success will work-only not to your favor. Your beliefs will create poor actions and that will deliver a result that is not synergized with your heart's desire. This does not reinforce the right set of beliefs.

For many achievers before your time, they had to trick themselves into success. Perhaps you have heard of the expression "fake it 'till you make it?"

Put another way, by acting "as if" you are already in the state you want to be in, your body, chemistry, and subconscious are fooled into thinking you are already lean, energized, wealthy, or happy. Faking a positive attitude may be uncomfortable, but it works! In fact, you can prove it to yourself this very instant.

Think of the happiest moment of your life. Capture that moment. Remember who was there, where you were, what you were doing. In your mind's eye, actually go there. Smell the smells of that moment. Listen to the voices of people you were with.

As you relive that moment, your brain is firing the same neurons it did when you experience it. In fact, put a smile on your face.

Put a HUGE smile on your face right now as you read this. Do you realize it is physically impossible to be happy and sad at the same time? As you relive this memory, in that very instant, your body, mind and feelings are happy. Sure you could switch to a sad moment if you choose to, but your mind cannot hold two feelings at the same time.

And you are in control of it.

In his younger days Wally Emery was not only healthy, his

• • •

"You have to expect things of yourself before you can do them."

~ Michael Jordan

• • •

health was a public examples to others. People aspired to be as "in shape" as Waller Emery. His awards included;

- Mr. Muscle Beach,
- Runner up to Mr. Universe
- Finalist in Mr. Europe competitions
- Black belt in Tae Kwan Do
- 1st Dan Black belt in Tang Soo Do

Wally was the ultimate picture of health. In fact he exuded health and fitness. As a competitive body builder his belief was clear; exercise=success.

As Wally got older he became less athletic and more sedentary. He began to put weight on and with it came health issues such as diabetes. Before he knew it this man, who had once been the figure of fitness was now overweight and sick. He had sunk into poor diet and exercise habits and was quickly spiraling downward.

Wally had a wake-up call that was life-changing. It was the proverbial lightning bolt of insight. An event transpired that didn't just shake him up. It nearly killed him.

The formerly healthy body builder had a massive heart attack.

The prognosis was not good. In order to keep Wally alive, the doctors performed quintuple bypass surgery. His very existence was now in question. Incredibly, Wally made it through surgery. However his doctors warned him about his poor health. They recommended that Wally make some substantial changes to his diet and fitness.

Without these changes he wouldn't stand a chance of living.

Wally dug deep into his soul and there he found his original belief – the belief that he was fit and healthy. He had suppressed it and ignored it for years, but it was still there. Wally took his ability to believe in himself and used it to fuel his comeback. He started to workout. He totally changed his unhealthy diet and replaced it with a healthy one. He began to shed the excess pounds he had put on from years of a sedentary lifestyle. Wally's doctors were astounded. Wally dropped the excess body fat and regained his self-esteem. He began competing in body building events again and his confidence returned.

Wally's comeback wasn't complete, of course. He didn't want to just be healthy, after nearly dying, he decided it was time to truly live. Wally was awarded the "Inspirational Grand Champion of 2002" in the Body-for-Life contest. Wally now is able to use his amazing story to inspire others who have been dealing with challenging health and diet issues. He is living proof that with new beliefs (or even past ones) you can connect to the proper action and deliver the results you want. In Wally's case, it was a matter of life and death.

Do you need to nearly DIE in order to change your beliefs? I hope not. Fortunately, beliefs are free. You don't need to be a former Mr. Muscle Beach in order to become one.

Like Wally, all of our beliefs are temporarily borrowed from an array of sources. With borrowed confidence comes new actions that will give you the life you deserve.

Our brain believes something and acts in accordance with that belief. That action generates a positive outcome that reinforces a belief. When that outcome affects others (It always will), the experience of those people reinforce our goal and the entire process spirals up When we have a belief that is disharmonious with our actions, we go nowhere or worse we go somewhere we think we're going but we're really not going there.

What happens to your beliefs if you have a peanut butter and jelly sandwich, two candy bars and a liter of diet coke when you are done working out because you have "earned it?" I've heard people say, "I worked out all week this week and I lost a whole pound. I'm going to reward myself with a bowl of ice cream."

That's stupid.

That ignorance makes no sense from a nutritional standpoint; it's idiotic from a belief standpoint. And, it certainly won't hold up on the action-results model. Our belief system is messed up. Why would you reward yourself of something negative?

• • •

"You can have anything you want if you will give up the belief that you can't have it."

~Robert Anthony
Best Selling Author

• • •

Because you don't BELIEVE it as being negative, you see that bowl of ice cream as a positive reward for your efforts. It's not. It's a negative reward. Our belief system is incorrect.

Game over. You'll never create the permanent change you desire.

In order to get your belief system in the right category, you've got to assault your current beliefs with new ones. In order to change your outcomes or change your results, you got to start with a borrowed belief. This is the reason most of us spend our entire lives "trying" to accomplish something. This is why only a fortunate few achieve super success. Getting your beliefs in line is critical. When your beliefs are misaligned you have poor results.

When we expect bad things to happen, don't they seem to pop up more often? If you're fan of the movie The Secret, you understand what I'm talking about. "The Secret" may seem new age, but it isn't. The concepts discussed in that movie really have been around for millennia. The appendix contains several ancient books of wisdom that spoke about these ideas long before man had the capacity to even make a film. The law of attraction and expectation is as verifiable as the law of gravity. There are people in your life right now that may not be as positive as they could be. They are negative, depressed, and when you see them they're complaining all the time. Now, I'm going to prove to you why when they say, "life isn't fair," or "my life keeps getting worse," this isn't simply an attitude. Their life really is worse! And it is a direct result of their expectation.

Suppose Debbie Downer complains all the time, she's depressed, she's not feeling well, she lost her job, and she's getting divorced. It can be pretty difficult to look on the bright side of all of that, of course. This is a really bad case.

You approach Debbie and ask, "Hey, Deb, how are you?" For the next 10-15 minutes (Which feels like an eternity) she dumps her entire litany of woes upon you. Your immediate thought is, "Hey, have a great day. I got to go." You want to get away from her. You're a positive person. You are physically removing yourself. You're taking an action to remove yourself from that negative energy, from that negative talk that he is putting out not just the universe but into your brain.

Now, you think you're the only one that thinks this way and acts this way? Nope. Other people who are positive, productive and successful are avoiding her, too.

Who does she end up talking to? Birds of feather flock together, right? Other people who are empathetic or sympathetic with her will say, "Yeah me too. Yeah, I know what you mean. That boss is a jerk. I had him as my supervisor for three years. I'm so glad I'm out of that department. Too bad for you. I feel your pain."

The result is Debbie's belief and outcomes are supported. Does she get new and better information and opportunities? No. Why?

The reason Debbie isn't afforded new and better opportunities is because all the new and positive opportunities are the property of positive people. It's not that we don't like to share them; it's just that we don't waste them with people who cast them aside as foolish "Pollyanna" thinking.

Debbie doesn't attract right thinking and good opportunities because she doesn't give any. I am not judging. It's just the way it is.

When you have the expectations of good things, you attract good thoughts, good people and good results. When you have the opposite of that, when you expect bad things, when you say you've had a rough year or tough time, you're going to attract more of that. Not through the ether of the universe necessarily although that probably is true as well but from the physical manifestations of the people you associate with, the books you read, and the information **you** put in your head.

When you're depressed, without controlling your thoughts and feelings, you tend to stay depressed. A body at rest tends to stay at rest. When you are thinking bad thoughts they tend to keep spiraling down. You must assault those negative thoughts and attack those destructive ideas and remove that filth from your mind. Defeatist thoughts and negative attitude drain your spirit and kill your potential. Destroy them with positive thoughts. In fact, a positive thought isn't enough. Your beliefs must be converted entirely. That's why stories are so critical.

Belief

"Before the decade is out, we're going to land a man on the moon and return him safely to the earth." This was a famous quote from John Fitzgerald Kennedy, and this was in the early '60s when the average computer was a size of a gymnasium, and the previous several years there's a bunch of fireworks going off at NASA where all the rockets exploding on launch pads and this crazy president wants to put three guys in a capsule and send them to the moon and back.

Think about it.

At that time, there was absolutely zero technology, achievement, belief, or expectation that we could put a man in orbit let alone to the moon and back. JFK was not a rocket scientist. Did he have the knowledge to do it? No. Did he have the affirmations to do it? Not really. One man can't affirm himself to the moon and back.

He had belief.

JFK helped us, inspire us, motivate us to put a man on the moon and return safely to the earth. Achievements happen because of expectations and belief. Of course you will create the action and gain the right knowledge to manifest it, but do you believe great things will happen in the future?

Dreamer

Dick Tracy was a popular cartoon that originated in the 40's. At that time, there was no such thing as a cellular phone. Even by the 70's nobody would have conceived of a cellular phone the way we have it today.

Or did they?

Conceiving of the vision and having the belief is where reality is created. You cannot create an object without first thinking about it. Does that make it "unbelievable" to conceive of a 2 way radio or TV that you could wear on your wrist? There is a linear progression between fantasy-possibility-reality.

In the case of a 2 way wrist radio, it was definitely in the realm of fantasy in 1941. Even as late at the 80's, when cell phones became more commonplace, there was neither the technology, nor believability that it could become a reality.

That was not the case for the engineers at LG electronics. In their minds, if it could be conceived, it could be believed. Now it is reality.

The logical extension of this process is that someday someone will develop a cure for cancer.

Do you know who that person is? I don't.

That future has not been written yet. But you're going to help write it. Your story of achievement is going to be shared with at least one person. You will have a chance and opportunity to share it with the world. Your story may motivate somebody to cure cancer. Even if you are not directly involved with the ignition of that dream, you're part of the web of influence. You're part of the fabric of inspiration, expectation and belief that's it's going to happen.

Chris Gardner had a hard childhood. Born in Louisiana in the early 1950's the family moved to Milwaukee when he was little. Raised in an abusive home he witnessed his stepfather beat his mother. At about the age of 6 his mother tried to fight back, setting fire to the house with his stepfather inside. His mother was sent to prison for four years and Chris was sent to live in foster care. He lived a rough childhood surrounded by events that would be traumatizing to any child.

Chris never realized he was the product of a troubled childhood – at least he never let it dictate his future. He knew that he was destined for success, for greatness. A defining moment came while watching a championship college basketball game when he was 16. It occurred to him that the players were going to go on to have successful and lucrative careers. If they could do it so could he.

After a chance meeting in a parking lot Chris was determined to become a stockbroker. In fact he can't explain how, but he just knew that he was going to be a successful stockbroker.

Well, Chris went through many ups and downs. He married but his wife left him to care for his young son alone. He didn't have a job and was even homeless for a time. No matter what his circumstances were, he continued to persevere in his belief in himself. He knew that he would be a stockbroker – even when it seemed to be a totally hopeless dream.

Today, Chris Gardner runs one of the most successful brokerage offices in Chicago. You may have even seen Will Smith play the part of Chris in the movie, "The Pursuit of Happyness."

Chris Gardner's belief was not an acceptance of his reality. His belief was of a future of comfort and abundance with his son. He didn't have a plan "B" or a back up scenario. It isn't enough to hope for a better future. In the case of Chris Gardner, he put everything on the line to create that future.

No plan "B"

Start changing your attitudes and beliefs. Let's begin with removing the word "try" from you vocabulary…forever.

The reason most people fail when trying to lose weight is NOT because they are on a bogus weight loss plan. The majority of plans that a reasonable person enrolls in includes the two basic functions of reducing the caloric intake and increasing caloric output. Everything else associated with that plan are peripheral gimmicks to help you stay focused. People fail because they have inserted the word "try" into their vocabulary.

Let's do a quick experiment. Take 2 seconds right now and raise your hand.

Did you do it?

Seriously…just do it. Raise your hand. I know it seems silly, but you'll get it after you read the next few paragraphs.

Now, "try" to raise your hand.

Did you do it?

Yes? No?

What happened?

"Do or do not. There is no try."

~Yoda

The essence of our thoughts is that by inserting the word "try" into any sentence structure or thought pattern we are giving our brains and our bodies an out. We are saying that failure IS an option!

You have failed at your past attempts to save money, get out of debt, lose weight or be a rock star because you tried.

Of course, other reasons may include choosing the wrong vehicle, road map or support system. However, even if you don't HAVE a car, you can always get out and walk. Your journey isn't dependent upon having a vehicle. It is dependent upon a commitment to getting to your destination. Of course, a vehicle can get you across the country a lot faster than walking, but we are not talking about speed-just victory.

Eliminating the word try is not just positive talk. You are wiring yourself for the option to fail every time you use it. I am sure that when Gene Kranz, the mission controller for Apollo 13 realized that his crew was in danger of dying in space, he didn't tell his staff to "try" and save them. In the movie, Apollo 13, Ed Harris, playing Gene Kranz looks at his staff. They all have the look of defeat upon their faces. Nobody said they couldn't save them, but their demeanor, attitude and internal self-talk was already contemplating the deaths of the Apollo 13 crew. Kranz instantly noticed the look of impending failure and commands his staff to erase doubt and the word 'try' from their vocabulary and their thoughts.

Failure is not an option.

Is it just a phrase or do those words have the power to save three lives and move a nation to a standstill?

It's been said that attitude is everything. Of course that isn't true. You can have an extremely positive attitude, but if you don't DO anything with it, you won't create any action. However, WITHOUT the proper attitude, whatever you do won't be as effective without it. Put another way, positive thought without action is wasted; action without positive thought is ineffective.

Attitude

Your attitude is going to be one of the biggest assets you have to help you reach your goal. You need to believe that you can reach your goal – believe it in your heart and soul. If you picked up this book to just get a little inspiration or motivation you need to pay close attention to what I'm going to tell you in this chapter. The main thing you're going to need to do is commit to training yourself to thinking, not just different, but better. Your life is a series of events. How you deal with those events, your attitude towards them, is a choice. In Buddhist doctrine, suffering IS part of life. It is not even an option in the beginning. The four noble truths put it very succinctly:

The Four Noble Truths

1. Life means suffering
2. The origin of suffering is attachment
3. The cessation of suffering is attainable
4. The path to the cessation of suffering

I am not going to convert you to Buddhism or proselytize to you. The point is that nobody can escape some degree of pain, suffering and tragedy in your life. You are going to lose loved ones. You are going to have setbacks. You are going to have challenges in your life. There is no escaping pain.

Since avoiding pain is not an option, what are you going to DO about it? It is human nature to instinctively avoid pain. Following a painful experience, physical or mental, rarely ends with the event. Pain is temporary, but our brain pulls the feelings of pain to the surface.

We try to avoid it, justify it or blame others for it. Behind your reaction is your attitude towards it. Any grief counselor will tell you that your tragedy is painful and you cannot avoid feeling bad about an unfortunate event that befalls you. Once that event has transpired, what do you do? For many people, anger, rage, resentment and blame consumes them.

A "bad childhood" or a debilitating car accident can emotionally scar a person for life. Healing those scars can happen quickly or not at all. This process for dealing with your emotional pain IS in your control. When it occurs, it might not feel like it, but the faster you can make this mental shift, the happier you will be and the faster you can USE the tragedy to your benefit. Spinning your attitude from negative to positive not only makes you feel better (and quicker) but it fuels your subconscious with strategies and tactics to overcome it and depending on the circumstance, actually BENEFIT from it. The more rapid your recovery, the quicker your brain stimulates recovery, renewal and creativity.

Without action your attitude is irrelevant. Right now one of the biggest fallacies in our self-help culture is PMA – positive mental attitude.

"If you think you can do something you can do it."
"Attitude is everything."
"Whatever the mind can conceive it can achieve."

Yes, but not without action to back it up!

The popular book and movie, "The Secret" is about the law of attraction and expectation. Using the law of attraction and expectation will create the abundance and prosperity in your life.

Put your thoughts out into the Universe and they will magically appear to you. Wow!

I've got news for you – That is only step 1.

Positive vibratory thoughts alone won't help you reach your goal. Of course having a positive mental attitude is a necessary component in the path towards achieving your goal but it won't work all by itself.

Positive mental attitude is vital, of course, because taking action without having PMA is a sure way to set yourself up for failure. Your mental attitude and beliefs must work with your actions. Without having a positive mental attitude it's like saying to yourself "I don't really believe I can do this but I will try anyway" It's like telling yourself that you'll give it a shot to see what happens. You are not fully committing to your goal. Your chances of succeeding when you use that kind of attitude are nil.

Imagine if you were to use that kind of attitude to enter the Olympic Games. Let's take exceptional achievement as our example. Do you think that they can achieve success using pure will or pure action alone? An Olympic athlete without attitude is a non-starter. Conversely, attitude without action doesn't do a whole lot either although it's a start because attitude without action at least gives you a starting point, which is hope. Hope is a first step to achieving anything. Without hope your mind speaks one language while your body speaks another and the universe looks at that as a mixed message.

It is important to start with a winning attitude. Start with the attitude "Yes – This is what I want. I **believe** I can do it, let's get going!" Once you do that things will fall into place more quickly for you and you will attract the right type of people into

• • •

"Looking for the positive effect of every event of your life is difficult, but not as draining as accepting the negative feelings of that event."

~Doug Crowe

• • •

your life. You see a positive mental attitude plus action plus accountability gives you a chance to succeed. Positive mental attitude plus habits plus feedback can give you the successful outcome you desire. PMA plus action plus accountability will create habits that will bring you towards your goal.

This onslaught of negative vibratory images and words is constant. This underpinning of negativity can create damaging negative thoughts and feelings. Even when we say something positive it may have negativity associated on some level. We need to rephrase our words and our very thoughts into positive ones. If you say you want to end abortion it's different from saying that you are pro life. While on the surface it may seem the same there is a negative connotation to the first statement.

Mother Teresa was once asked why she didn't participate in anti-war demonstrations. She replied, "I will never do that, but as soon as you have a pro-peace rally, I'll be there." While it may sound like the same thing there is a clear difference between the imagery and intent of the statements. One statement is negative while the other is positive. War has a negative feeling while peace has a positive one. Mother Teresa put a positive spin on the situation.

Overcoming the Negative

Your attitude is important not just to maintain the status quo between negative influences and positive ones, but to create a new framework for you to live by. This will become more than a habit. It will be your new framework for thinking, dealing with and acting on every situation in your life.

I know that sometimes people who are positive *all* the time can appear irritating – I'm sure you've come across some of them. If you've listened to people like Tony Robbins either you love him or you hate him. He is so positive and so energized all the time he can wear you out. By keeping yourself focused on the positive of every situation it will become second nature to you.

Your own self-talk is going to help you on a continual basis as well. You're going to have to work yourself so that ongoing self-talk will continue to be supportive. Be aware of all the things that can have a negative effect on your attitude – your friends, family, environment, society, economy, etc. Be aware that you need to battle these negative, depressing and unsupportive streams of information.

You also need to battle your own negative feelings. You may have feelings of guilt or of being unworthy. You must remove these negative feelings and replace them with positive self-talk. Remember – you're only with your spouse for a few hours a day, with your boss for eight hours a day but you are with *you* for 24 hours a day, 7 days a week, 52 weeks a year for years and years. You have the most control over your thoughts and luckily you also have control over yourself. You must learn to retrain your brain.

Retraining your brain takes patience, it takes perseverance. Psychological studies have shown that it takes about 17 positive thoughts to knock out just one negative thought. Unfortunately you can't just do it one time. You need to continually replace negative thoughts from your mind until your subconscious can take over and do it for you.

In order to create permanent change, you will seek out and absorb a continuous stream of supportive thoughts, knowledge and feelings. This constant stream of energy on autopilot is what makes Express Lane to Success different than other books. Our accountability system at Bexsi™ will interact with you on a daily basis giving you a steady supply of supportive positive thoughts. The system automatically delivers:

- A power planning workbook customized to your personality.
- Automatic emails with a short motivational story.
- Automatic text messages reminding you of your action steps.
- Daily affirmations via voicemail.
- Listen from your 'future self' about your abundant new life.
- A fellowship of support via our achiever's network.
- 1 on 1 power partner who holds you accountable.

You'll soon see your own success story unfold as you grow and get closer to your goal. You'll experience the positive effects not only in your life, but your family, friends and the world around you. Your experiences affect the world.

Attitude is not knowledge, information is not attitude, and even our beliefs aren't really attitude. Attitude is an underlying foundational feeling of success – of being positive. It can also be negative if we allow it.

When you have the right attitude you can transform your circumstances. You can't change the past – this isn't a time machine. But what you can do is take a look at the past and find out why things happened the way they did. You may say "Wow that really knocked me for a loop" or "That experience caused my bankruptcy". You will learn that the attitude you have towards an event will shape your very destiny. So while you can't change the past you can use the past in a positive way to create a new and prosperous future for yourself.

People often say that it's not what happens to you – it's how you deal with it that counts. Similarly, when dealing with other people you can't change the other person. You can't make someone stop shouting at you, you can't tell someone to stop feeling the way they do. What you *can* change is your attitude –

• • •

"You cannot control what happens to you, but you can control your attitude toward what happens to you, and in that, you will be mastering change rather than allowing it to master you"

~Brian Tracy

• • •

the way you react to the other person. All you really need is attitude to make changes in your life.

Jessica Cox is a remarkable young woman. Her story is one of hope and teaches us that attitude is important in reaching your goals. While you may think that there is nothing extraordinary about a young woman getting her pilot's license her story is far from ordinary. You see, Jessica Cox was born without arms. Jessica's parents were dismayed and heartbroken when their only daughter was born – with no arms. While this may have deterred most people from getting anywhere in life it had quite the opposite effect on Jessica.

Growing up Jessica learned to use her legs and feet as arms and hands. While she had prosthetic arms she found them clumsy and hard to manage. She grew up with incredible drive and a strong belief that she could do anything that she set out to do. She didn't let her "disability" stop her. In fact, she doesn't really consider her situation a disability. She learned at an early age to use what she had to her advantage. As a young child she imagined herself flying over the sandbox taking her young friends with her. She now sees what her imagination can accomplish.

Jessica is an inspiration to us all. When she decided to learn to fly it took her a considerable longer time to learn. She manages all the controls with her feet. She truly is a living example of how a positive attitude can help you accomplish anything you set your mind to. Jessica says "Never let your fears get in the way of your opportunities". Besides piloting an airplane Jessica helps inspire others. She gives motivational talks to young people and always aspires to do more. She hopes to someday teach others how to fly. Jessica has done more than most people without any disability.

Obviously Jessica had circumstances that most of us can't imagine. Even having been born without arms is not something that happens often, thank goodness. For this young lady her attitude was everything. Without her positive attitude there is no way she could have learned to text with her toes. Without that attitude there is no way she would have even hoped to learn to fly an airplane. Without that attitude she would have been dependant on others for everything for the rest of her life. Was attitude all-important? No, because attitude without physical manifestation of that attitude to put the plan into motion would not have helped either.

How did Jessica know that she was going to be able to learn how to fly an airplane without any arms? The answer is – she didn't. The answer is that her unshakeable belief and her ability to accomplish anything she sets her mind to is what she had. She used it to the fullest extent of her potential.

Can you say that about anything in your life? The full extent of your potential has not even been brought to bear.

Do you think it is difficult to learn to fly an airplane without any arms? You'll be even MORE SHOCKED to read the rest of the story. You see the plane is 100% unmodified in any way.

If you think flying is tough without arms, you'll be flabbergasted at Jessica's next goal. After you spend some time being impressed with an armless pilot, all of your excuses will disappear when you read her next goal.

Jessica's next adventure is even more unimaginable than flying. To read more, go to www.bexsi.com/2 now.

Section II

~ Action ~

"The self is not something ready-made, but something in continuous formation through choice of action."

~John Dewey
Founder of functional psychology

Chapter
Four

• • •

"Positive thought without action is wasted; action without positive thought is misguided."

~Doug Crowe

• • •

Self-Talk

If I was to tape record your thoughts on a daily basis, what would I hear? Would they be positive, negative, or neutral? If you could somehow record every single thought in your head every day for a week, what would you record? When it comes to achievement, there is a clear and definite distinction between those who achieve and those who do not. The main difference is how they communicate with themselves. We all have two voices in our heads; one that says, "You can do it" and the other that says, "You've tried that before...why don't you quit fooling yourself."

If you could actually record these voices and play them back, you would hear both sides justifying their position, giving you reasons, excuses and ammunition to support their battle. In the battle of overeating, you have said, "One Oreo can't hurt." When you start a part-time business in order to set aside money for retirement and the cash doesn't flow in the first 6 months for you, you may have said just before you quit, "This doesn't work."

Like the proverbial devil and angel on your shoulder, there are two voices constantly at odds with one another. On one side, you have the optimist who is creative positive and sees a bright and successful future for you. The other voice is more insidious...this voice ALSO sees the future; only it justifies procrastination, wrong action and negative affirmations.

Your positive self (PS) is the one we most want to listen to. PS is exemplified in the rising of the sun, a warm summer's day and a job well done. When we watch a powerfully emotional movie with a happy ending we have given energy to PS. Think back to the last good story you read or watched. Most likely it had a hero who had fallen, been beat up and rose above the challenges to become a better person or contribute to the world. It is a very common theme in movies and goes like this:

Chase the hero him up a tree.
Throw rocks at him.
Rescue him.

You can apply this 3 part saga to movies such as 'It's a Wonderful life', 'Rudy', or any uplifting television show or fiction book. Redemption from the pain and suffering of human existence is a compelling theme. It resonates with our sense of hope, purpose and our sometimes our very existence.

It fuels Mr. Positive self, your PS.

Why then, have you failed at your last attempt to reach a goal? Why hasn't old PS come to YOUR rescue, saved the day and carried you off to a happy ending?

Then answer is painful, but simple.

There is another voice inside your head. Your negative self (NS) is sneaky. Your negative voice can speak to you in more than one language and has more fuel than PS. NS comes at you when you aren't expecting and constantly is supported by the exterior world. NS has the experience of reality to back him up and defeat PS. NS is poison.

Every time you watch the local news and see who killed whom, you support the imagery of negativity. Every time a friend tells you the economy is rough and times are hard, unknowingly gives NS more energy and power.

The negative self-talk that goes on in your brain is the voice that has lines that have been memorized and repeated back inside yourself day after day for years. These lines are so extremely powerful, that your body often creates an environment and reality to support them.

"You can't do it that fast."
"I am surprised you think you could be like that"
"Not everyone can be a millionaire"
"I am just big boned"
"You are too old"
"You are too young"
"That's too dangerous"
"You are too late"
"You are too early"
"Nobody does it that way"
"You've tried that before"
"We've always done it this way"
"Are you sure that's a good idea?"
"One more XXX won't matter"
"I can start again tomorrow"

Of course there are thousands more questions, phrases and statements that reinforce negative thinking and the resultant negative outcomes. One of the worst versions of this is when you actually win the battle with NS but lose the war with your goal. You may have taken the action required to make a positive difference but the results are too far into the future.

For example; you begin an exercise regiment and for 2 straight weeks you are consistent. You 'feel' better, but the results you expect don't appear. This plants more doubt in your belief system and causes a decline in your attitude. This, in turn, can reduce the passion in your action which weakens your results.

Spiral down B.A.R. results.

The problem with this long term scenario is that without any current reinforcement in the present day, you are fueling PS only with the 2 dimensional hope and vision of a better tomorrow. There is no concrete evidence of your accomplishment. THAT is when NS creeps into your head and begins to chip away at your goal and the actions that, given more time, would actually create the outcome you desire.

When it comes to big goals, time is not on your side.

Athletes are a prime example of this passionate self-talk that they use to become winners and champions long term. Ask any gold medal Olympian if they visualized themselves standing on that podium months and even years before they actually did it. They spoke to themselves daily during training. The conversation in their head continuously spoke of achievement, success and positive comments. Their internal dialogue was rich with the assumption of winning. Their self-talk was purposeful, deliberate, positive and effective. They literally spoke their destiny into existence.

In order to defeat your negative self talk, you must take a multi-pronged attack on it. If you don't unleash all of these weapons, you may be re-reading this book a year from now "trying" to make your goal happen...again. Each day take a moment and check off your application of these 5 tools to reinforce your positive self talk and destroy your negative self talk. This is an ongoing mission and there is no "end date." You will have to battle this voice for the rest of your life. At first, it may be difficult, but after a while, you'll actually enjoy it! Below are 5 activities you must do on a daily basis.

Affirmation your future in the present
Reduce the volume of negativity
Short-term rewards for yourself
Increase the positive with 3D power
Read supportive examples

Affirmations

Affirmations are serious mind games. Affirmations are audio and are visual representations of your future self. You may scoff at the affirmation exercises presented here. Like many people before you, you may say they are silly, stupid or simply aren't worth the embarrassment. Unfortunately, as you will experience, affirmations are already a significant part of your daily routine. The difference is what you have told yourself up to this point has brought you exactly where you are. You are already affirming your beliefs-the wrong ones.

Put another way, "You are where you are because of your thoughts, what you believed and what you did."

Nobody wants to hear your excuses about the abused childhood, bad economy or glandular problem. Those kinds of excuses may take the sting out of the wound, but the results are the same. Do you want to improve? Good. Then eliminate excuses from your vocabulary and replace them with possibilities.

Let's use the incredible power of your subconscious mind and affirmations to take firm control of your life and your destiny. Instead of using affirmations to support your excuses, we are going to use them to add fuel to your vehicle and place you clearly on the Express Lane to Success.

Chicken or the egg

You probably know the riddle, "Which came first? The chicken or the egg?" Certainly, you can't create an egg without a chicken to lay it and you can't create a chicken without it hatching from an egg. While this riddle may frustrate children, adults realize that question is flawed. There is no finite point of beginning.

The same is true for your transformational change. You will find many of the exercises, affirmations and visualizations untrue. Telling yourself you are thin when you are not is a lie.

Telling yourself you want to be thin, when you don't believe you can is also a lie. Do you "think" before you "act?" Even my own B.A.R. model is a circular model. Your achievement has no beginning. It is a process like the evolution of a chicken. You don't have a specific starting date. You are not "fat" you are not "poor." You are inside a circular loop of change.

Your only mission is to create a framework of belief inside that loop that supports a new and better future. This can only be done by "priming the pump" of thought and telling yourself you ARE lean and you ARE wealthy right now! By starting there, your brain and body will begin to work together towards manifesting the reality of those thoughts and actions.

For now, set aside any linear framework on your Express Lane to Success. You'll need to lay an egg right now and hatch a new affirmation of the person you see for your future.

By creating an affirmation system, you'll be like a car wash; putting your dirty car through it every single day. Our minds get dirty; our minds are assaulted with negative, irrelevant and ridiculous information. Who cares who won American Idol? I don't care, it's pure entertainment, but I know people who know every single Idol winner and the songs that they have won. They put this information in their brains, for God knows what.

We all need down time but not at the expense of achievement!

What if they would take that same amount of time, half hour a week and affirmed who they were going to become? Instead of watching somebody else become the number one singer in America, what if they visualized <u>themselves</u> becoming the number one in whatever they do. Add in a good dose of applause, encouragement and an affirmation of that success and you can bet that you'd be living your dream right now.

You can start today.

You have the ability right now to change your thoughts and to affirm who you're going to be-who you were meant to be. Too many people are pushed and pulled throughout their lives by fear, greed and circumstances. Most people don't realize that these forces cloud their judgment and pull them off track on a daily basis.

Our lives are the sum total of our days, so make **this day** special.

You not only need to push out irrational fears and eliminate negative greed from your thoughts, you need to supercharge your new affirmations. Your brain is more powerful than all the supercomputers in the world-combined. It is the most complex array of connections in the existence of the universe. There are over 100 billion neurons in your brain and of those neurons there are over 20,000 connections in any combination of those 100 billion neurons. You don't have to be a math genius to understand my point.

10 billion to the 20th thousand power is a big number. It's the number that represents the most complex computer in existence. The processing power of your brain is capable of 38 thousand trillion operations...per second.

The most powerful supercomputer in the world can only perform 92 trillion operations per second. The means that the most powerful supercomputer in the world (IBM's BlueGene supercomputer) has .002 percent the power that you have between your ears. You would think that with all that incredible power, that "fooling" your brain with an affirmation would be difficult-even impossible.

Even though we still haven't characterized the true nature of memory and our mind, we do know how to trick ourselves into success.

An affirmation is a simple form of mind control, hypnosis, or a Vulcan Mind Meld. Affirming thought or action is a reinforcement tool that can transform indecision to decision. Over time, with enough affirmations and evidence to support those decisions, the question of "do or do not" is removed from the equation. No longer is a decision required. Your action is automatic. You've developed a habit. You've won.

Consider the last emotional movie you saw. Maybe you loved the movie "The Notebook" and were all choked up and even cried a bit. My favorite example is "E.T." (We can lean all about life from the movies!) E.T. created a bond with young Elliot and when E.T.'s friends came to take him home, I would be willing to bet that you got a little choked up and perhaps had a wee bit of extra moisture in your eyes. With the music flowing and the characters welling up in emotion, it is difficult not to get caught up and get a little emotional yourself.

Here's the bad news for your brain.

That extraordinarily complex supercomputer with it 100 trillion synapses, somehow created a chemical reaction in your body. Those synapses fired and created a lump in your throat, a permanent memory in your brain and tears to well up in your eyes. That supercomputer somehow can't distinguish between a real tragedy and a beam of light blasting through celluloid portraying the separation of a boy actor and a rubber puppet.

Yeah...your brain is the most advanced supercomputer in the universe but it is STILL easier to fool than telling your 4 year old about the tooth fairy.

Even though our brains can create the technology to put a man on the moon, for some reason, it can't distinguish between reality and fantasy. Of course, poorly portrayed fantasy can be set aside in our brains as pure entertainment or escapism, but given the proper input of music, images, and environment, our brains can easily be fooled.

The same is true regarding the past and future. When you look at an old photo album, you recall memories of your past. Your synapses fire and recall the dusty memories of that experience. Your conscious brain remembers it as an experience of the past. Your subconscious brain, on the other hand, is out of your control. If I were to put those images in 3D, add some music, clear all distractions and suspend your disbelief, I could cause the same neurons to fire in the EXACT same sequence as when those experiences actually occurred.

You can trick and influence your subconscious with as much ease as raising your hand.

In 1987, professional performance expert, Tony Robbins was hired to improve the marksmanship for the US Army. "The basic qualification at that time was 'Marksman', with 'Sharpshooter' and then 'Expert' coming above that - a Marksman being able to get 30 hits on target out of 45 rounds fired. Two groups of soldiers were taught side by side - one group getting the NLP-based training, - the 'control group'- getting the standard army training.

"The control group took 27 hours to get 73 per cent of the soldiers to Marksman level, with only 10 per cent of the group making Expert. The NLP-based group took 12 hours to get 100 per cent of the soldiers to Marksman level, with 25 per cent making Expert."

Mr. Robbins described his method of NLP (Neuro Linguistic Programming) of getting the recruits into a "state" where they recalled the feelings, breathing, body language and all sensory inputs that the very best shooters had when they were at their best. By modeling the attitudes, beliefs, physiology and breathing patterns of the top marksmen, new recruits were able to improve their scores significantly. What does this have to do with affirmations? How can you apply this to your goal?

Simply put, we are going to trick your brain.

You may not have the Hollywood budget of Steven Spielberg or the experience of Tony Robbins, but the good news is you don't need it. In order to use the same technology to improve your performance and create the proper skills and habits of the super successful, you will give yourself visual, auditory and experiential affirmations.

You are going to trick your brain by telling it you already are successful. By giving your brain the same stimulus, the same beliefs, attitudes, and physiological states of the super-successful, you will essentially re-wire it to make it IMPOSSIBLE to fail. Let me bold that for emphasis.

By modeling the attitudes, beliefs, actions, physiology, associations and knowledge of the super successful, you will reprogram your brain to achieve whatever you want.

You will be able to win-every time.

You will have to craft specific affirmations for your specific goal. When I did this exercise in 1994, I selected an affirmation from Zig Ziglar's book, "Over the Top." This affirmation rewired my brain for success. It allowed me to become the number 2 sales representative at my job at a national communications company. (#1 spot went to my good friend who had an advantage...he was an immigrant)

I printed this affirmation up, embossed it in plastic and read it to myself every day-out loud. Reading to yourself is acceptable behavior. Reading out loud is normally reserved for children and the mentally insane. In fact, since you will be repeating these affirmations out loud DAILY, you may very well be perceived as insane.

You may want to do it in private.

(NOTE: Bexsi™ members get these cards printed with their names on it, laminated and shipped to them in 2 sizes; wallet and planner)

Take a 3 x 5 card and print or write the following:

I, ____________________, am a courageous, caring, compassionate, humble, teachable, optimistic, conscientious, hard-working person. I take genuine pride in my appearance and performance. My self-image is good and is getting better because I am a dependable, confident, motivated, bold, and personable. I have an excellent sense of humor and am a pleasure to be around. These are the qualities of the winner I was born to be and today, I am using these qualities in my personal, professional and family life.

If you are serious about making PERMANENT changes in your life, you'll actually take out a card, laminate it and throughout the day, read this ALOUD to yourself (when appropriate...keep it in private or risk being labeled as a raving lunatic).

The passion and volume you read this will react in direct proportion to its effectiveness. The more passionate you read this every day, the more it will be engrained into your conscious and subconscious. The louder you read it the more you will believe it. The more tonality and resonance you feel when you read it the more real it will become. This will create the results that you truly want. In fact, it will help you squash the negative self talk that is there. That battle is never ending.

For a specific goal, insert specific milestones and achievement points that you desire in the following. I would suggest that you put one (or all of these on separate cards) on the back of the previous card.

Health

I, _____________________ am a fit, trim, energized and healthy person. I am at my ideal weight and I am a high energy person. My diet consists of nutritious whole foods and I am a great example for my friends and family. I only have one body in this lifetime and I treat it like the temple that it is. I fuel it properly with the nutrition that it needs and exercise it accordingly. I love my body and am admired by others for keeping it at peak operating condition at all times. I am healthy.

Finances

I, _____________________ am a responsible, achieving, financially secure positive money magnet. My income exceeds my expenses on a monthly basis. I am clearly aware of the opportunities around me and carefully consider them before investing or spending my hard earned money. I believe there are infinite amounts of wealth available to my family and me. I acquire wealth easily and give just as readily. I live in abundance and know I am destined to have as much wealth as I desire.

Relationships

I_____________________ am attractive, charismatic, valuable, personable, healthy, and engaging individual. I possess the qualities necessary to attract and give love freely and openly. I am interesting, fun, smart, playful, athletic, sexy, warm, courageous, and attentive. I am an exceptional catch for a person who appreciates my qualities. My relationships are positive, engaging and the people in my life all are better off because of my spirit.

All of your affirmations must be spoken in the present. You must act, speak and visualize your new life as though it has already happened. Remember, with enough stimulation, the brain has no sense of time. With enough inputs of auditory, visual and experiential points, the brain can release chemicals and feelings today of an event that occurred years ago (Or even an imaginary event of an alien befriending a boy in Los Angeles!)

In addition to speaking your affirmations in the present tense, it is critical to only use the positive word of any negative situation. You should never say, "I want to be free of debt" or "I want to lose weight." By stating your affirmations in the positive sense, "I live in financial abundance" you don't allow any room for your sneaky negative self to get a toe hold on your plans. Even the hint of a word like debt, even though the words "elimination" preceded it can be dangerous. It may seem a minor difference to you, but to your subconscious mind, clarity and positive thought are all that matter. Good intentions aren't enough.

All of your affirmations must be spoken with a positive spin and in the present tense. By speaking in the present tense, especially when you look into the mirror, you will feel a twinge of guilt-you are lying to yourself. Here's a fresh perspective on how to get over that feeling and how to literally trick your mind into believing the future is now and that you body, finances and relationships are primed, prepared and owed the health, abundance and love you deserve.

Remember the chicken or the egg example? Since there is no clear starting point to the creation of a species, likewise, there is no starting point to the creation of the new you. Your body, mind and spirit is never static, never does it literally start or stop. Even in birth or death, the energy that we are is merely transferred or changed. It is a known law of physics that matter cannot be created or destroyed, it merely changes form. Your form is constantly changing. The difference TODAY is that you are not going to experience one single day from now on, without an awareness of your absolute control over your destiny, your life and today's thoughts. By creating a new thought...right now, you are shaping and creating a new future. You cannot believe with 100% certainty that you are a healthy individual, without acting in accordance with that belief. By acting in accordance with that belief, you create the results of that belief.

You aren't lying to yourself.

You must take the element of time out of the equation. Your conscious mind is aware of the passing of hours, days and weeks. However, do you notice how 2 dimensional the past is? When you look around you right now, do you see how clear, vibrant and 3 dimensional your surroundings are? The present moment truly is, all that we have. Your past is vague and unclear. Your future is also an unclear variable that can change at any moment. You have your hands on the wheel. It is time to steer it. Choose a direction and put your foot on the gas.

Speaking your future in the present tense tells your subconscious mind that all is well and that you are ALREADY thinking and acting if it is reality. The power of your subconscious is a powerful weapon in your arsenal. This attack on your negative self is important and vital to your success. Be aware of it every day. Reflect on your thoughts and actions constantly.

Believe in your new future and act as if it is already here.

It will be uncomfortable only for a short time. By speaking in present tense, your actions will support these affirmations and your new reality and achievement will come at you faster and clearer than ever before. It is what professional athletes and super achievers do on a daily basis and you are now joining this league of extraordinary accomplishments. I know it is odd to talk to yourself like this. The first time I did it, I was embarrassed. It felt extremely awkward. Believe me, it gets easier.

The first time you do ANYTHING it is awkward. Your first date, your first day on the job, your first step as a baby; these were all awkward moments the first time you did them. But, like all things, the more you do them, the easier they become and the better you get at them. Coincidentally, the more they become your reality.

It's about to become weirder.

Visualization

Speaking your new life into existence requires effort. Tricking your brain to cause a tear in your eye requires a multi-million dollar Hollywood budget or a repetitious affirmation. But simply affirming your future in the present tense isn't enough. You are on the EXPRESS lane to success, not the slow lane. In order to get there faster and with increased confidence we are going to borrow some strategies from Hollywood. You need to visualize and when appropriate, experience the new success in your life.

Visualizing the new you will require a touch of creativity. When you consider the new you financially, physically or emotionally you need some visual representation of that person-that life. You will need to revisit 7th grade again because you are now required to do a poster.

You need to create a poster of your future. Clip out images of health, wealth, prosperity and any visual representation of the life of your dreams and glue it to a poster board. Put this poster on your desk or on your refrigerator. The daily reminder of where you are going and what you want will reinforce your subconscious brain consistently. It is through this constant imagery that allows your subconscious to work its magic. While you are sleeping or at rest, your subconscious continues to work and your beliefs seek out solutions to the problem.

What problem?

The problem that your brain "sees" a present situation of what you desire that is incongruent with your reality.

Do it now.

You've begun the habit of reinforcing your future through auditory affirmations. Now you must create visual representations to solidify your future. Over 80% of what we learn is through our sense of sight. Even our words speak in pictures. When the word pink elephant is written here, you visualize that pink elephant. Even an intangible word like love conjures up a vision in your mind. It could be the vision of a mother and child, your spouse, or two people holding hands walking along the beach. Regardless of the words, our mind always thinks in pictures. This is why abstract thought are more difficult than the discussion of material things. Being a better "you" is abstract. Measuring and quantifying it is exceedingly difficult and open to massive interpretation. We don't need your negative self to interpret a brief achievement or short-term win as a better you. This could sabotage your journey and achievement of your goal. In order to give you conscious mind something to work on while you work, sleep and play, you are going to burn into your cerebral cortex the images of the new you. These images will be clear, quantifiable, measurable and represented visually.

Health, Wealth & Joy

You are either at peak physical health or you are not. If you are, you don't need to read this paragraph...move on. If you want to be in better health, it is time to create a visual representation of the body you want. If you have ever been fit and trim in your life, find a picture of that and paste it onto your poster. Even if it was 12 years and 3 kids ago, you once had a body you could be proud of. It doesn't matter that you are middle aged or your body has changed. Our bodies are a mass of cells that grow, divide, die and are replaced on a consistent basis. Your epidermal skin cells only last about two weeks until they are replaced. Blood cells-about 120 days. Your epithelial cells-your gut...those guys don't even last a week until they are replaced. With an average life span of 5 days, you are replacing them on a constant basis.

What's the point of this scientific update, you ask?

Your body is renewing itself constantly. You are going to insert new knowledge into your thoughts and those cells, when replaced have the same DNA as before, but they will be renewed in a new body, with new beliefs and you will be thinking and acting as a fit healthy person, so your cells will respond accordingly. Take any photo of your fit and trim past and paste it to your poster board. You are going to renew that body to the size it knows it can be. It's done it before. It can be there again.

What if you've never been fit and trim? Like so many people born into an environment of overweight or obesity, what can you do? I am not going to lie to you; it will be more difficult for you.

Someone who has never been thin will have a harder time visualizing BEING thin. They have no framework, no reference and no memory of that body. It is more difficult for you and that is the cold, hard fact.

It is also an opportunity.

Inside your body is a lean, fit and energized body. Your simply have excess padding that is masking what is inside. As you look into the mirror and see the excess weight, look again. This time, as you look at yourself, visually remove that excess fat as if you are removing a coat.

You are not overweight. You are lean, fit and trim. The only difference is you have an EXTRA layer that must be removed. The more you can clearly visualize yourself removing that layer, the easier it will be for your body to act "as if" and begin a healthy strategy of nutrition and exercise. If you have never been thin you will be using the examples of others to give you the proof, confidence and belief that you can do it, too. Examples are a common and popular standard for learning. As it turns out, it is necessary for you to use examples from others regardless of your history.

Just as you are not going to depend on any one tactic to accomplish your goal, nor will you use only one visual reinforcement tool to re-wire your brain for attainment of your goal. Visualizing the new you through pictures of success, health and prosperity come in many flavors.

Get a picture of a person who is your age and gender that is fit, trim, healthy and idolizes the image you would like for your body. Don't settle for average. Go for it. You may or may not attain the absolute peak of perfection, but as you know, nobody does. However, by having a visual representation of what you are working towards you will continually bombard your visual cortex with images of health. When this visual is from another person, we say in our mind, "If she can do it, I can do it."

This is the fundamental reason stories of overcoming challenges are so inspiring to us. Someone born with a silver spoon in their mouth who achieves greatness ticks us off. A person who overcomes all the odds against them and succeeds is revered, even though both people might have achieved similar pinnacles of success.

On your journey to create a better you, reading stories of success from people who have overcome great challenges will help you. Don't ever stop doing it. Reading an inspirational story or book, like "Chicken Soup for the Soul" does wonders for creating a grateful heart and a renewed spirit. Even watching a good movie like "The Rookie" or "Rudy" will do wonders for inspiring us to achieve. There is a list of inspirational movies in the appendix of this book. Even if you've seen some of these before, we all can use a pick me up now and then. Go ahead and let the positive side of Hollywood create a chemical reaction in your body. Those endorphins can be put to good use.

Do the same exercise for your finances, your relationships and any area where you want to see improvement.

There are some personality types (You know who you are) which are modest and are not comfortable with putting material objects on a board. "Wishing for riches" is a symbol of greed and excess and it is seen as disingenuous. That is absolute nonsense. Prosperity can come in any form YOU decide. If you are not turned on by money or the things money can buy, you are not better than anyone else; you simply have enough to be comfortable. I won't criticize you if you don't criticize me.

The pursuit of money for money's sake, of course, doesn't work. In fact, not many people actually think that way. The large percentage of mature, even modestly educated adults realizes that their pursuit of extra money is really a desire for the reduction of stress. Would an extra $100,000 in the bank take some of that stress away? How about $500,000? Of course it would reduce some of your stress. Funding a child's college tuition or your own retirement are noble efforts and visualizing that by putting pictures on a poster board will be a positive reminder of why you are working so hard on yourself and your goals.

Your ideal home, vacation, lifestyle, hobby or financial freedom can be visualized by putting pictures of a sun-soaked beachfront, a beautiful home, or your favorite car are good starts to imprinting your brain with the visual reminder of who you are becoming.

The act of visualizing your future is not an option. Visualizing success, fame, fortune, or even something as simple as drinking a cup of coffee is required before acting. It is impossible to perform an action without first thinking about it. Your conscious brain is not an involuntary muscle. Visualizing something as simple as raising your arm to bring that coffee mug to your mouth may not seem like a tremendous feat (Whereas NOT bring that 2nd cookie to your mouth is!).

However, consider that there are thousands of synaptic messages that must be relayed back and forth between dozens of muscles in an orchestrated movement to perfectly time the operation so you balance the mug, retain your grip, open your mouth at just the right time, pause your breathing so as not to choke and engage your tongue and mouth muscles in perfect unison is actually quite extraordinary. It doesn't take an extraordinary amount of visualization, but you are a pretty advanced organism!

Visualizing something as monumental as maintaining a healthy weight or living debt free can seem overwhelming, but to your brain, it is the same. There is no difference in magnitude to raising your arm to take a drink or creating other movements, actions and habits to re-structure your lifestyle.

To your brain, the functions are identical.

To your negative and positive self, however, it is a different story. That is why visualizing your future is required. If you can't visualize the end result clearly, your brain won't act in congruence with your body and you are doomed to fail. You see, it's not even your FAULT that you are overweight, in debt or not living the life of your dreams...it is your brain's fault!

The good news is also the bad news, of course. You are in charge of and 100% responsible for the thoughts, knowledge, belief and attitudes of your brain. When you control and direct it properly, the actions will follow and your "chicken or the egg" question will no longer be relevant. The answer to that question is "both." The chicken didn't start out as an egg or vice versa. It was a process that evolved over time and so it is the same with your process of achievement. You are starting from a point in the present and you must constantly live, breath and believe in the future. By living in the future, you are destined to achieve it. Of course the corollary is true. By living in the past, you are doomed to repeat it.

Visualizing your future and imagining it as your present day life may appear as idiotic as speaking your affirmations aloud in the present tense. However, we are not done visualizing your new life just yet. There is one more step you must take to imprint your brains thought patterns with your new life. This exercise will take you off of the written word, beyond the visual reminder of your future and put you squarely in the experiential re-wiring that you need to guarantee your success.

You must taste it.

Now before you think I am going to suggest you go out and lick the bricks on your new home, relax. This stuff may be odd, but there is no activity that will get you really committed to the loony bin.

Just as there is a difference between praying by yourself or with your congregation, there is a difference in thinking and talking about a new you and actually experiencing it. When able, you must use ALL your senses to create your new vision.

Physical Association

You may not be able to actually feel what it is like to be 50 pounds lighter, but each time you shed 2, 5, or 10 pounds, you WILL feel a difference. Once you have accomplished that milestone-relish it. Take just a moment and create an experiential anchor that will create the feeling, physiology, memory and thoughts of that moment and burn it into your brain. When you hit that milestone, look in the mirror; slap yourself on the back and shout, "I look GREAT!" By slapping yourself on the back, you have created a physical anchor to that moment. Repeat it a few times and say over and over to yourself, "I look GREAT!" This anchoring of audio and visual reinforcement along with the action of a slap on the back can create a constant anchor that you can use in the future.

Like Pavlov's experiment with salivating dogs, a future slap on the back will remind your subconscious and conscious mind that "You look Great!"

If your goal is for an increase in finances, freedom or relationships, you are already thinking, believing and acting "as if" it was already there. The visual reminders of your lacking however continue to give power to your negative self talk. Here's a trick that can knock that guy out for more than just a few hours.

Suppose you live in a modest home that is old, cramped and need of tremendous upkeep. Your vision for financial independence is living in a brand new home with lawn service, a 3 car garage and no upkeep. You can see your kids having their own bedrooms and a backyard where they can play safely with the neighbors. In fact, that neighborhood is just a mile away from the dilapidated shack where you live now. Here is what you do:

Walk by that neighborhood every day. Visit an open house whenever you can. When you get a chance to go inside, don't simply say to yourself, "what a beautiful home" start to visualize what it will be like to live there. Imagine your kids coming home with their friends and having a safe, clean environment to play in. Create the vision of what it will feel like to have professional yard service, a nanny or any luxury you can dream of. Don't be shy. It is your life and your future is unwritten.

You are writing it now.

By placing your body in the exact atmosphere and environment that represents your financial independence you are tricking it. By telling yourself this IS your life, you are letting your subconscious mind know what it feels like to live that life. Since your subconscious doesn't have a sense of time, it begins to arrange itself to live in that world. If the world (your health, wealth and happiness) isn't actually in that world, it begins to move you in the right direction to align everything. Put another way, your true beliefs both conscious and subconscious cannot exist in a world that is not aligned. Just as two objects cannot be in the same place at the same time, your true thoughts cannot believe one thing and act out another. Thoughts and actions are connected.

Your chicken laid an egg.

THAT, dear reader, is the reason we spend SO much time on your thoughts! If changing your life, habits, patterns, and behaviors was easy, the entire world would be debt-free and healthy. Your thoughts must act in accordance with your true beliefs. You cannot act wealthy without being wealthy. You cannot act healthy without believing you are healthy.

You can't even have a sincere smile or laugh when you are angry.

Investing in subverting limiting thoughts, negative ideas is going to be a habit that you will carry with you for the rest of your life. If you haven't been a positive person before, the best time to start is today.

By honing your skills of communicating with yourself first, you will be able to win at everything. By affirming the new you along with speaking your future into the present, you will believe, act and perform within the top 1% of those whom you admire and are modeling.

Want to be as fit and trim as an Olympic athlete? Start thinking, acting and living like one. Is that too lofty a goal? How about simply being fit, trim, energetic and healthy? Does a person who fits that description drink to excess? Does a person who is fit, trim, energized and healthy eat junk food, fast food or processed foods on a daily basis? Does that person exercise? Do they ACT healthy?

Yes.

By believing and acting healthy, you will become healthy. Is that too simple?

"But Doug....I am 50 pounds overweight and tired all the time. I am stressed about my finances and my relationship with my significant other isn't any better? I can't look in the mirror and say those things with any amount of honesty," you say to yourself. How can you look in the mirror and state your healthy weight in the present tense, while looking at yourself knowing you are not at that weight? Doesn't the reality of the mirror trump the lie of your words?

That's true. But your mind is easily fooled. It takes repetition, patience and a multi-pronged strategy to create the new you. When doubt creeps in and your NS tells your PS that you are NOT what you are saying, remind yourself of the circular reference. Which came first; the chicken or the egg?

Eliminate the linear sense of time to overcome the barriers of your present reality. Think in a circular fashion.

Since your subconscious has no sense of time, use it to the fullest extent with your affirmation process. Affirm your goal in the present tense. Write down the goal as if you have already achieved it. Writing the results of your goal, who benefited, and how it feels will "trick" your mind into making it a reality.

Use pictures, live examples and the repetition of positive self-talk to create an environment of success. You have the tools necessary to achieve your goals. Why not use them all?

Projecting yourself into the future isn't easy. The future has so many forks in the road. There are infinite choices. Any one of them can lead you to prosperity and an equal number of them can send you back to where you started-or worse.

Back to the Future

In the movie, "Back to the Future 2", the obnoxious Biff Tannen, steals a sports Almanac from Marty McFly. Biff as an old man (future) comes back from the future and has a conversation with his younger self. He instructs him to take care of this almanac so that he can bet on all the sports games and become insanely wealthy, which he does.

What if your future self could have a conversation with who you are today?

Take a moment and imagine the PERFECT life. Your health, finances and relationships were all absolutely the way you wanted them. You have all the financial resources you need to provide for your family, charity, retirement-the works.

What it would feel like to have a near perfect body. You are limber, lean, strong and energized. You get compliments from your peers daily on how good you look. When you look in the mirror, you aren't vain, but proud.

What would it feel like to have a social life that was ideal? You relationships with your significant other, your family and your friends couldn't be better. You give and receive love as easily as you breathe.

Where would you live, what car would you drive and where would you vacation if money was no longer an issue in your life? What would financial independence mean to you? How much would you like to donate to charity? What would it feel like to have absolutely no debt whatsoever?

When you create these images, do not treat them as a fantasy, but as a reality. Picture the sounds of your day, the smells of the healthy meals being cooked in the kitchen, the vacations you take and the peace and joy of every day of your life. Imagine this IS your life exactly 5 years from today.

Project yourself fully into that future. Turn the volume up on the music in your stereo. Turn up the volume on the laughter you are having. Create the visuals in 3 dimensions. Make them vibrant colors. Put all the people you love into your vision.

Now, take a single day from that life-a snapshot. You walk onto your back porch as the sun is setting on the ocean. It is the early evening hour and the air is crisp and the temperature is perfect. The sunset has created a brilliant orange glow in the sky and you are completely calm and relaxed. You are living that life and you take a moment to reflect upon a single day in the past. This one day was your moment. This one day, galvanized in your head as clear as the present, was a single moment 5 years ago. You smile and remember that fork in the road you took. You reflect on a single, simple decision you made 5 years ago. You thank yourself over and over again for taking that significant fork in the road. You remind yourself that you had a rough few years, but you got back up, dusted yourself off and started over. You empowered yourself with a new attitude. You read better books. You eliminated watching irrelevant TV programs. You thank yourself for making the permanent switch in your diet and exercise program.

You thank yourself for that day in the past, which coincidentally, is today.

What if that person, 5 years in the future, could travel back in time today? Like Biff Tannen in "Back to the Future 2", what if the future 'you' came back right now and told you a single secret about your future.

Imagine if the perfect future 'you' could come back, whack you on the side of the head and remind you of what you HAD to do today in order to create and sustain that near perfect future. Would you listen? Would you complain? Would you ignore yourself?

Sometimes these exercises may seem odd. Trust me, the clearer you project your future; the more likely it will become your reality. If a fit, successful and totally happy 'you' could come back today and talk to you, what would that future 'you' say to the present 'you'?

What would a happy, successful, energized, healthy future YOU say to the person you are today? You can create a time machine like Doc Brown did in "Back to the Future" with a simple tool we have at www.bexsi.com. This tool will send you a voicemail from the future 'you' to your life in the present. Log on and send a message to your present self from the future you!

Chapter Five

• • •

"The world makes way for the man who knows where he is going."

~Ralph Waldo Emerson

• • •

Stop Setting Goals

Instead of working on making more money, losing 20 pounds, or reducing alcohol consumption, your first step is to develop the tools to become a better person. You will create, write down and commit to a goal achievement system. However, without laying the foundation of the proper skills to attain it, all the perseverance in the world is useless if you foundation isn't established.

In order to transform yourself into a fit, wealthy, energized, charismatic success-the envy of your peers, concentrate on developing specific attitudes and skills.

Ignore your specific goal for a moment.

Before we establish your specific goal achievement system, reflect on the qualities you need to develop on a daily basis in order to become more efficient, positive, and energized. By embracing daily motivation messages, thinking clearer and being on the top of your game on a daily basis, overcoming your obstacles (a critical strategy of this goal program) will be easier.

When you can embrace your values, clearly define your roles and hone your interpersonal skills with yourself, you will be prepared to create the life of your dreams. Your new set of skills will empower you to accomplish any task, gain any advantage, and create infinite possibilities within yourself. Becoming proficient at using these tools will be a lifelong passion.

Goal Setting – Everything You Know is Wrong

The Express Lane to Success is about achieving your goals. Your attitudes, character and wisdom will change and work together to create a blueprint for your life, but planning and *executing* the steps requires action. Setting goals is one of your first action steps towards achieving them. With hundreds of books and systems to choose from it is no wonder goal setting is one of the most misunderstood and misused concepts in the history of performance. Most of these programs are very good. So why is it that most people who have set goals failed re-set them and failed over and over again?

Setting goals is easy-right?

Many goal setting programs profess that all you need to do is to think big, write it down, set a date for accomplishment and you will magically achieve it. When you take the time to sit down and put your goals in writing you are among the 1% of people who actually do that. Of course simply writing a goal alone doesn't ensure your success.

Everyone knows that you have to actually DO something-right?

Any reasonable person knows that a goal without any action is merely a fanciful dream. You will do much more than simply write them down, you are going to anticipate obstacles, plan how to get through them, and be accountable to your actions. You will have a plan of execution and a system to measure it.

People who dream without a plan, purpose, support and action will continue to dream without attaining their goals. As the driver of your new vehicle and since you are an Express Lane to Success achiever, you are going to do MORE than simply plan your goals. You are going to take all the necessary, awkward and even painful steps to insure their success.

What is the difference between someone who hopes for success, who tries to move ahead and the person who has it all? Does the super-successful achiever have a magic formula? Were they born with more luck? Do they have a predisposition to wealth, success or achievement?

There is a story that has been floating around for years. This urban legend says that in 1953, researchers surveyed Yale's graduating seniors to determine how many of them had specific, written goals for their future. The answer: 3%. Twenty years later, researchers polled the surviving members of the Class of 1953 -- and found that the 3% with goals had accumulated more personal financial wealth than the other 97% of the class combined!

The moral of this story is:
1. Goals work.
2. Almost nobody uses them.

Why you must set goals

Anthony Robbins aptly points out in his books on goal achievement that "success leaves clues". The study of success is a great strategy for designing your own future. Are there any new ideas out there, as yet uncovered? Certainly, there are innovators in the world of achievement. You can study and analyze people like Abraham Lincoln, Michael Jordan, and Mother Teresa who have set new standards for achievement. However, when you deeply scrutinize HOW they did what they did, as opposed to the achievement itself, you will discover that they all shared the same strategy and tactics to make their dreams come true. In addition to thinking RIGHT and having unshakable belief, they set and committed to a specific goal.

You must set a goal in order to achieve it. The evidence is clear as it is depressing. Millions of people, people just like you, have dreamed of small, medium and even large goals. People just like you have hoped and dreamed of a better life in one way or another, and because of their LACK OF A PROPER STRATEGY, those dreams died within them.

Define your goal

What is it that you want to achieve? Remember not to speak in the negative. Don't write what you don't want. Don't use words like "get out of debt" or "quit smoking." These phrases contain the very subject that you want to avoid and eliminate. Your subconscious mind doesn't comprehend time and it isn't very good at English, either. Oftentimes your subconscious hears the word "debt" and filters out the words "get out of" from the phrase. This leaves the word debt in your brain. As you go about your day, work, play and even sleep, your subconscious is always working. It doesn't have a lot to do, but your subconscious mind will be working out problems, creating ideas and aligning these forces together. Remember, your conscious, subconscious and actions cannot be at odds. In order to become a super achiever, all of these powers must act in alignment with each other.

By clearly defining your goal, your mind creates a three dimensional vision of your future. The clearer your vision the more likely it becomes reality. Here's why:

With an infinite amount of variables in your life, you have unlimited roads to choose from when embarking on a goal. You don't live in a vacuum. Your life is not only your private experiences. Even if you are a hermit in a basement, your life impacts the universe by your thoughts and actions. Since everyone has unlimited paths before them, the combination of these paths is infinite squared. It is like taking the flat, 2 dimensional world of a desert, with 360 degrees of direction before you and putting it in a 3 dimensional world of space…the variety of choices before you is compounded by the choices of others.

The more clearly and vividly you can define your goals the more likely you will achieve them. Clear vision has power. Vague generalities do not. When your goals are vague, other influences on those goals are easy.

If you say, "I want to make more money." As soon as you find an extra twenty five cents between the cushions of your couch, your goal has technically been met. Now you may not FEEL as though it has, but your subconscious mind recognizes it as a win. Remember how you felt when you pick up an extra dollar found on the street? Have you ever forgotten about an old savings account and when you re-discovered it you felt wealthier-if only for a moment? Your surprise and joy, however slight, gets an endorphin rush and your subconscious mind says, "Mission accomplished." Of course your conscious mind does no such thing, it is still agonizing over the $1,257 in unpaid credit card balances you have.

Vague goals have a zero chance of success not simply because your vision is vague. The thoughts, actions and interaction of others affect your actions. Without a clear vision, you will fail. Without clarity, you may get exactly what you want…mud.

Clarity

Here is a simple method to establish clarity of your purpose and a boundless set of goals to strive for.

Set aside a good chunk of time and a remove all distractions from your environment. Get out a few clean sheets of paper.

Write down 100 things you want to be, do and have in your life. Write down these things without any restrictions. Pay no mind to your health, finances, age or any other restriction. Write down as many experiences you would like to have, property you would like to own, languages you would like to speak and skills you would like to have.

Don't stop until you have at least 100 things. I have done this exercise with over 250 people and many of them tend to get stuck around number 66! Keep writing.

After you write down your 100 things take a look at the list and write down your 10 most important roles in your life in a column next to it - Father, husband, son, friend, businessperson, etc.

Now write down your values – God, country, money, family, etc. Take a look at your goals, roles and values and line them up. You will notice that many of your goals affect multiple roles and values. These are your first targets.

There will be combinations that will reveal to you that there will be at least 10 goals that have double, triple or even quadruple effect in your life, in the life of your family or even in the lives of people you don't even know yet. Those are the ones you're going to focus on first. Those are the ones that will have the greatest impact on your life. When you look at those 10 ask yourself one question:

"If I can achieve one of these goals in the next 12 months, which one would I choose?"

Some of the goals may look like 2, 5 or even 10 year goals. Some of them may be 3 or 6 month goals. I want you to look at all 10 and select the one that will have the biggest overall impact in all of your roles – the one that is supported by the largest amount of your values and that you believe is achievable in about the next 12 months.

If you register for the online portion of this book, you will be sharing your list with an accountability partner. You will be matched up with a person who has already achieved the same or similar goal. This is a real person, a person just like you – not some celebrity or fictional person that you can't really relate to or won't inspire you. You're going to have real two-way communication with this person on a weekly basis. Together you will pull from within yourself the power you need to achieve your goal. In order for this to work, of course, you must volunteer yourself to help someone else first. This is a pay it forward program – in order to get you've got to give.

So write down your single most important goal – one you believe can be achieved in the next 12 months – and submit it. You will be paired with a person who will be in touch with you on a consistent basis. They are going to help give you the confidence, support and belief you need in order to achieve the very goal that's going to make the biggest impact in your life and in the lives of your family.

Volunteer to be an accountability partner for someone else. By giving the very thing that YOU need, you strengthen yourself and you begin the process of becoming a more powerful goal achiever for yourself. You can view this as selfish or generous-in works both ways!

Balance is a Myth

I can ask you a question – "what's the most important thing in your life" and you may answer "God". Fine. My response would be, if God is the number #1 most important thing in your life, "How often do you pray?" You may answer "Once a week". I ask "How long do you pray?" and you answer "About an hour". Maybe you pray twice a week if you have a test coming up, right kids? Or let's say you are extremely faithful and you pray every day for an hour or two. That still leaves 22-23 hours per day to eat, rest, make a living, and spend time with friends and family. If God is your #1 priority, why wouldn't you invest a majority of your time with that value?

Some people may say that their family is their number 1 priority. If you have nothing else, you always have your family. Ok, then the same question applies. How much time do you spend with your family?

My point is that balance is a myth. There is no such thing as an equal balance amongst all the values and the roles you have in your life. You have multiple roles in your life. Almost all of us, at one time or another has roles such as:

Wife or Husband to Spouse
Daughter or Son to Parents
Employee or Employer to Company
Community Leader or Follower to Service Organization
Friend for Someone or Friend of Someone
Provider for Family's Finances or Home
Role Model for Youth, Church or Others

You probably can think of a dozen other roles that you are responsible for throughout your week and throughout your life. As you journey down your Express Lane to Success, of course, some roles will grow and others will shrink. The myth of a proper work/life balance isn't realistic because your life changes constantly. When a person is in school, they normally do not have to be a provider for their family, especially before they are 18. When you are a senior citizen, your responsibilities as a son or daughter should be about over.

In between those times, many of us feel more pressured to work and provide financial security, role model for our kids, stay in good health, make our parents proud, be involved with our community, and basically do EVERYTHING well all at once.

Forget it.

Your ability to manage your self-talk and develop high-impact habits is your objective. Without focusing on your performance skills, you will do ALL of the above roles at a mediocre level (or worse). All you have to do is look at the foreclosure, bankruptcy, divorce, suicide, drug abuse, and crime rates of our society and you can instantly recognize that our skills at becoming better individuals has not gotten any improved.

Developing the right thoughts and right action will create the right results.

Writing down a goal separates dreamers from achievers. Putting dates on your goals separates the goal setters from the goal doers. But, unleashing unlimited potential is reserved for those who have a positive spirit and an unbreakable will. If you remove the past from your dreams, your creativity is unlocked. By casting off the shackles of your circumstances, you empower your creative genius and ignite your super conscious power.

Using your values and roles in concert with your actions will exponentially increase the quality and speed of your achievement. Take a look at your goals, roles and values on a daily basis. The more you look at what you do, the more you can become who you want to be. There is no rule that says you can't be a good husband and a good father by achieving a singular goal.

Too late

One problem you may face when writing down your dreams is that some of your dreams are from a distant past. You may have wanted to be superman, an astronaut or a cowboy. As a middle-aged person with responsibilities, that dream has been pushed so far back into your memory that you may have forgotten it. This filter in your mind must be removed.

Most adults dream with filters in place.

Don’t make that critical mistake. There are thousands of examples of people who ignore those filters. The movie, “City Slickers” when the character played by Billy Crystal decides to embark on a vacation AS a cowboy is one example of removing your filter of responsibility, if only for a week.

Adventure travel, fantasy baseball camps, and eco-tours are all designed to appeal to our dreams.

"Well, no, Doug, I am 45 years old – it's too late for me to be an astronaut"

Really?

Do you realize Richard Branson is pre-selling tickets for space tourism?

I wanted to be a fighter pilot when I was younger. I am fortunate enough to have 2 very loving and inspirational parents. In fact, my inspiration for aviation came from my father was a pilot in the Army Air Corp (Before there was an air force).

I was mesmerized by his old uniform and the pictures of the WWII aircraft he flew. Even after he retired from the military and became a successful dentist, he continued to fly general aviation planes and nothing is cooler to a young boy than flying with your dad or hearing stories about his adventures of flying toilet seats to Alaska (Hey, I said he was a pilot…I didn't say he was a FIGHTER pilot!)

My dad inspired me to learn how to fly. Dreaming of flying a fighter pilot dominated my thoughts for years. The dream of flying for the military, however, would never happen because my eyes weren't good enough. It was a non-starter. The dream has zero chance of even being attempted.

Flash forward to 2000. I am 40 years old, Desert Strom was a victory and the pride in our armed forces was restored. On my 40th birthday I sat next to a fighter pilot who flew F-14s in desert storm and he and I went up in the sky in a SIAI Marchetti Italian trainer. It wasn't a jet, but I had a full day of actual air combat tactics (ACM) training with an F-14 pilot who had real combat experience.

My dream was fulfilled in one glorious day.

I spent the morning in ground school, learning how to attack, evade and manage airspeed, gravity and maneuvering. After our ground training and briefing, we took off in this trainer along with a second aircraft. The second plane had a friend of mine in it with his co-pilot. We spent a full day learning what it actually feels like to dogfight in the sky (without the chance of death!) The company, www.aircombat.com video tapes the entire experience. In fact, they hook up each aircraft with lasers and a smoke system to record each of our "hits." The entire experience is as real as it gets, without the danger of dying!

You CAN live your dream, folks. You CAN shoot planes out of the sky. You CAN be an astronaut, you CAN cure cancer – you CAN do anything you set your mind to as long as you don't quit. As long as you have the right system in place, you do everything I tell you and don't take no for an answer.

Remove your filters and dream.

• • •

"Hope without a plan, will remain a dream, never to be realized or appreciated by yourself or others."

~Doug Crowe

• • •

Dream BIG

Make no small plans. We are surrounded with conflicting messages. Work hard, work smart, become rich…right? Power corrupts, the rich are greedy, and who needs a 100 foot yacht, anyway? That money should be given to the poor…right? Maybe.

I was raised by an entrepreneurial father and an incredibly generous and liberal mother. The best of both worlds, I think. Work hard, do well, save for the future, but use your wealth to help out the unfortunate. Does it mean that you shouldn't desire a flashy sports car or a second home?

Of course not.

The yacht manufacturers and home builders love earning a living, cranking out the products you want. Consumption fuels employment, investment, and economic growth. The wealthy are also the largest group of benefactors in the country. When you achieve great wealth, you can have it all. You can help to employ thousands of people by owning a second home, and you can still donate to your favorite charity. Mark Victor Hansen once said, "The best way to help the poor is not to be one." So get over any guilt you may have about money. Go ahead and earn as much as you can. Dreaming big has value. Dreaming big creates more prosperity for everyone. Dreaming big is critical to your success.

By dreaming big you create more power for yourself. Big dreams are the stuff of legend. Big dreams attract partnerships, capital and passion. Your vision for greatness must, of course, reach beyond yourself. It is dreams that are larger than you that make the biggest difference. Dream big and you'll attract other dreamers.

Large goals have more power than small ones. Large goals will allow you to weather the storms that are sure to attack you. Large goals have more energy. Large goals survive. Small goals are easily crushed, destroyed or forgotten. Dream big.

There is an extremely powerful side effect of dreaming big. By creating big dreams, you catch the attention of others.

Large goals attract the attention of others. Small, personal goals are fine. They are critical for survival. But, when large, honorable goals are announced to the world, you attract attention. Some of that attention may be unwanted and negative. We'll deal with that later. The positive, supportive attention will give you a greater chance of success. Imagine a goal for achieving a million dollar net worth. You will get the support of your family, for sure.

If you set a goal for a 5 million dollar net worth, with using 4 million of that to build an orphanage, you will attract other resources to help you attain that goal. People, foundations, and money will come your way when your goals are honorable, large and selfless. Dream big. You'll attract the help, support and resources of other people.

Passion

Passion is the fuel for all goals. Without passion, large goals are impossible to achieve. Without passion, there would be no Mona Lisa, no space shuttle, and no IPod. Without passion, large strides in human achievement could never exist. Without passion, no great deeds are possible. Therefore, in order to get what YOU want and to make minor or significant changes in your life, passion must be a component of achieving your goals. Remember, this book is not about setting, but achieving your goals. While planning is an integral and necessary part of goal achievement, without passion, the negative forces that pull you away from your goal have more power.

Most often, these negative forces are people.

"Who would want to sabotage my goals?" Well, depending on the goal, there are always external forces who doubt you. There are always friends, relatives, or associates who tell you outwardly or in a subliminal manner that, "it can't be done." There are always forces at play who innocently (or maliciously) try to bring you down. Passion, commitment and the unshakeable confidence that you have in your goal is your primary weapon you need to vanquish the forces that are at odds with your goal.

And that weapon needs constant sharpening-daily.

Of all the negative forces attacking your goal, there is one that is the most powerful. This single force doesn't attack your goal once in a while, but every day and sometimes every hour. Often times, this attacker isn't overt. The attacks are disguised as relaxation, excuses or 'do over's.' This force will be with you forever and has currently been stronger than you. This combatant is infinitely harder to recognize and doubly hard to eliminate. In order to relish your passion for your goal and to perpetually feed that passion the fuel that it needs, you must learn to acknowledge debate and destroy the one sole power that can kill your dream quicker than any negative boss, friend or relative.

It is your internal voice - your self-talk.

How does a person who is in perfect health act? How does a financially successful person think? What does a person with loving and nurturing relationships do? What kind of thoughts, actions and interactions do you need to do now, in order to create that new you?

Your journey into your future begins with thinking, acting and interacting as a successful person thinks, acts and interacts. You cannot expect results before putting forth the belief and action. In this circle of success, your chicken and egg are right in front of you. By putting both your thoughts and actions on a parallel course of success, you will travel on your Express Lane to Success in excellent financial, physical and emotional health.

Join the convoy and get on our "on ramp" to success at www.bexsi.com.

Chapter Six

• • •

"Obstacles don't have to stop you. If you run into a wall, don't turn around and give up. Figure out how to climb it, go through it, or work around it."

~Michael Jordan

• • •

Obstacles

Dreaming big will help you clear large obstacles. This is a major reason to dream big. Small dreams are problematic. When small dreams face medium-sized obstacles, the obstacles will win.

YUK!

Imagine a small compact car hurtling head long into a large brick wall. The outcome is not going to be good for the car. Your small goal (small car) will most likely face some type of obstacles. Life happens. Anyone who has been around for any length of time has faced obstacles. How we deal with those obstacles determines the quality of our life.

Now, imagine that you are driving a large, semi-trailer truck at a brick wall. Even at a modest speed, that wall is going to lose the battle. At a high rate of speed, you may not even notice a tremendous amount of deceleration. The obstacle will be obliterated, and you will be happily motoring along (even with some slight damage). This is one area of goal achievement that I have not found in very many books, systems and goal setting plans. It seems that with all the positive attitude books and new age "thought energy" talk that some experts believe that thought and positive energy alone can bring you to Nirvana.

Reality check, amigo.

You WILL have obstacles. In fact, your obstacles both internal and external are the reasons you are reading this book now. While a large percentage of your energy and new information is being focused on re-wiring your self-talk, attitude, beliefs there will still be external forces that will block your road to success. You will never be able to anticipate all the obstacles that will be placed before you. Developing specific tactics for anticipated hurdles is almost always a waste of time.

Suppose you had a goal to lose 2 pounds of excess weight this week. Based on a hypothetical, doctor approved plan, you map out your tactics.

First, you prepare a week's worth of food that had 40% less carbohydrates and 80% less sugar than your normal diet. By your calculations this would reduce your caloric intake by 25% for the week. Next, you are going to walk an extra 2 miles per day that you aren't walking now. This will increase your caloric burn by 5% for the week and your super duper plan will result in 2 pounds coming off in 7 days. You don't cook daily; you plan this out with detail and prepare an entire week's worth of meals and/or have them scheduled with whatever system you are focused on. Your strategy is backed up by your doctor and you are pumped!

Monday and Tuesday go perfectly. You are eating better, your energy level seems to increase a bit and for the first time in years, you feel you are on the right road to success.

Tuesday night you get a call that you have to fly out the next day for an emergency meeting. You book a flight and are across the country by noon on Wednesday. You have lunch with a client and save the deal. That evening your branch office takes you out for a celebratory dinner and cocktails since you saved not only the deal, but their jobs. You have a reason to celebrate; the deal not only saved their jobs, but guaranteed your quarterly bonus of an additional $2,000. You are on cloud nine. You have a drink to celebrate with the staff...then another. Desert menu comes out and even though you don't order, Bertha Butts on your right orders your favorite triple chocolate lava cake and you share it with her. Your glycemic index spikes, the bill arrives for $2,317, you have a massive coronary and you drop dead.

No, that's too morose. Your glycemic index spikes and you feel stuffed and don't die suddenly.

But you do die slowly and earlier. Why?

Because you can't stick to your tactics of the prepared meals you did so diligently on Sunday evening. You relied on tactics instead of strategy. Your plans were thwarted by a legitimate last minute out of town trip. You try a NEW tactic of starving yourself the next day. Your body stores fat as future energy. You don't lose any weight and you quit. Tragically, you resign yourself to the idea that you are big boned and while you don't die suddenly, your body ages at an accelerated rate. You develop diabetes in 12 years and your life is miserable. You failed. You focused on a tactical approach to weight loss. You believed that your tactics were sound (they were). However, like all heroes of famous battles, all the planning in the world is tossed in the garbage as soon as the first shot is fired. All military successes are based on superior strategy as opposed to finite tactics.

By focusing on your STRATEGIES as opposed to your TACTICS you can win.

List Your Obstacles

List each of your challenges, obstacles and anticipated hurdles. There should be an increased number in relation to the size of your goal. Don't worry too much about these obstacles. No achievement of any size was faced and accomplished without facing and overcoming some obstacles. You WILL have them. It will be easier to face them on paper with a plan of attack then at the moment they happen. Planning for failure is not a bad thing as long as you have a plan to overcome that failure. When you outline your solutions for each challenge, be sure to list several solutions for each one. You may find yourself engaging one, two or more of these solutions until you find out the perfect match to make your obstacles disappear. Remember, large goals of worth will benefit more than just you, so talk with the other people who will benefit and ask for their input. The synergy of two or more minds creates more creativity and energy than you all by yourself.

Get help.

Honorable, important goals will be attractive to anyone who shares your values. Don't be shy. Share your dreams with others. You never know how they can help. In fact, by posting them on the Bexsi™ achievers networking site for free, we can all help each other in creative solutions to our challenges. When you announce your passionate, worthwhile goals to the world, you will attract the resources, both human and other, to your cause.

Be sure to list appropriate strategic moves to overcome your obstacles. While you may list tactics, without a sound strategy to support the tactic, you will lose. Assign target dates to each step. Without those dates, human nature being what it is will let you off the hook. Procrastination can set in. Put those dates down in ink and commit to them. DON'T fill in the date achieved section until you actually achieve the task. Make some tasks ongoing and others with a definite end. Your goal may require the help of others. Don't forget to engage that help. This form is useful for small, medium or large goals. The action steps can be weekly, monthly or longer. For optimum results, you must have daily action steps that move your goals forward (however slowly) on a consistent basis.

Reward yourself

Just like training your pet with a snack, human beings respond well to rewards. Ask anyone who is appreciates their Christmas bonus or a person on a diet plan who loses their first 2 pounds. Human beings thrive on recognition and reward. As a self-directed achiever, you are responsible for rewarding yourself for achieving your own goals. If you hit a particular financial goal that you are proud of, take a small percentage and reward yourself and your loved ones with that special dinner, a vacation or new car. Just make sure the reward is commensurate with the goal. Don't set a goal to earn an additional $25,000 and spend $20,000 on your reward! 10% is a good benchmark for rewarding yourself. The satisfaction of many goals cannot be measured in dollars and for those intangible goals; you will have to devise a proper reward that is positive, fulfilling and appropriate.

Learn a new language? Then go and translate for someone for fun.

Did you lose those additional 20 pounds? DON'T go out and have ice cream!

Pay off a credit card? Invest the difference into a savings account.

Utilize a positive reward that is congruent with your goal! If you attained a certain position at work, take your boss out for a nice dinner. Just be sure to relish in your success. Take those feelings and plow them back into your next goal. Like Pavlov's dogs, you'll be salivating for more.

Developing your internal mechanism for passion and drive is absolutely a critical component of your new success. All by itself, it may or may not work. But, without it, significant goals are unreachable.

Develop, create, and nurture your passions. They will carry you through the hard times, and give you the fuel necessary to carry you on the sometimes long road to achievement. When the negative voice of doubt, fear and worry rears its ugly little head, bash it down, put duct tape over its mouth and starve it to death.

Join our achiever's network for FREE at www.bexsi.org today.

Chapter Seven

• • •

"It is easy to dodge our responsibilities, but we cannot dodge the consequences of dodging our responsibilities."

~ Sir Josiah Stamp
British economist, industrialist and banker

• • •

Accountability

Lets explore the idea of accountability more closely. You are at point A and want to get to point B. Along the journey many things happen. Remember how many times you've tried to reach a goal in the past but didn't make it? Think back to when you were 13 years old and dream about being an astronaut. Then when you're 18 you attend college and maybe decide to become an architect. You study for that goal. By the time you're 25 and you've made 80 applications to architectural firms you realize that your real passion is in sales. You switch careers and get a job in sales. By the time you're 35 you've burned out in sales and realize that you hit a glass ceiling. Then someone asks you to be in management. Suddenly you're managing a sales team and before you know it you're 40 years old managing a sales team and realize that you gave up your dream to be an astronaut.

What has happened is on your path from point A to point B things have pushed you off your path. Some of those things were good for you – making money, raising a family, etc. Our destiny is not in stone. You may have multiple outcomes for your future and it is up to YOU to write them. We write it as we go along. Attitude affects the clarity, circumstances affect the path, health affects the timing, and our decisions shape the rest. Your knowledge, association, economy, family and friends are all pressures pushing you to the left or right, up or down, along your journey. You never really end up at point B in your life. You didn't even have a clear idea of what point B was.

Even if you are a true die hard "Director" personality and your destination is a clear as can be, you actions and interactions will shape and change that destination. It is similar to practicing trading in the stock market. When a person decides to start investing in the stock market, prior to placing their hard earned money on the line, a common strategy is to "paper trade" first. This allows theories or strategies to be tested hypothetically, first. The strategy looks like this:

- Learn about a specific industry or market.
- Place fictitious trades on paper.
- What would have happened if you had used REAL money.
- Develop your trading style, risk tolerances and goals.
- Paper trade again until you can develop consistent results.
- You are prepared to trade your hard earned REAL dollars.

You can paper trade in the stock market all day long but the moment you put your first dollar down everything changes. Your investment of real money, however small, has changed the dynamics of the market. You have actually affected the path itself. Even though destination "B" was clear, your actions on the path to "B" affected the path and therefore the outcome you were after.

This doesn't mean, of course, that all destinations are elusive. However, your actions will create an infinite variety of outcomes that affect the path itself. Clarity of the outcome isn't enough to make it a reality. A clear strategy is required as well. With a proper strategy, you will be able to persevere as the forces of change push you off your path.

By having an accountability system like Bexsi™, it will be easier to keep your eyes on the destination and not the immediate obstacles which can derail your efforts.

As long as you have the daily encouragement, positive thoughts and tasks to move you forward to your goal, you can focus on that goal and almost ignore the obstacles around you. Some people may call that myopic. Some may call that obsessive. Some obstacles are better classified as distractions.

Excessive TV watching, surfing the internet without a plan or answering emails every hour can derail your focus. You will be able to better manage your time after reading and applying the principles in section 3. Even seemingly large obstacles such as poor health or a recession, however, can be acknowledged, but almost ignored when you lock onto your goal. You are not going to allow anything get in your way.

Worth

Passion without value isn't worth much. The desire for money for the sake of money rarely works. In order for goals to be realized and for people to benefit, there must be **worth** involved. Nearly everyone dreams of becoming a millionaire. Striving for and achieving financial independence is not a bad thing, of course. The trick is making sure that you seek wealth for a purpose. Money is not the root of all evil. The "love" of money is. There are millions of happy, successful, financially independent people. There are also a plenty more who have large sums of money that are NOT happy. A conversation with the rich and happy reveal a startling fact. They have a greater purpose. Rich, successful and happy people tend to achieve great things because;

They have passion for what they are doing.
Their passions extend beyond themselves.
Their confidence is unshakable
They fully expect to win.

Financial independence is a great reliever of stress in a family. If you ask any self-made millionaire they will tell you that the elimination of financial stress from their lives releases massive amounts of creativity from inside themselves. They will also tell you that the pursuit of money was NOT the engine that drove them, but the pursuit of a dream.

You have locked unlimited potential to do more than imaginable. Unlocking your potential will be your ongoing mission. Being AWARE of your passion, inner voices and sense of giving will be your key to unlocking massive amount of wealth, health and happiness for yourself. The difference between great, historical achievers and the common man is the internal communication within themselves. Mastering the self-talk between your positive self and negative self is just the beginning. By rewarding yourself with small medals of honor and reminders of the small achievements, you'll carry yourself along the journey with increased confidence, awareness and speed. Is that all we need to battle the negative self-talk?

Hardly.

Character

When your character is proper when you do the right thing whether somebody is watching you or not and you act in accordance with that character the world will bend to your will. When you have the correct knowledge and you have researched the right things in your life and gotten that right information and acted on that information the world truly is your oyster. Attitude, character and wisdom are all important characteristics of winners. Character is the one trait that one that you will leave behind after you time on earth is done.

Jennifer Thompson was a model student, an admired daughter and the homecoming queen. Nobody expects to be attacked and raped. It always happens to the "other person." Jennifer Thompson was about to become one of those "other people." When her perfect life was shattered in a single night, the petite blonde with dazzling eyes became something she could never have imagined.

The perfect witness.

Police rarely see a victim so composed, so confident and sure. Just hours after her attack, after a physician tested her for semen samples and she sat in a police station, scanning mug shots and working up a composite picture. In the same evening, she picked out his eyebrows, his nose, his mustache. She picked out his photo. She had found her rapist. A week later, the police had picked up the attacker and she stared coldly through the one-way mirror, "That's my rapist."

Ronald Cotton and he was the same age Jennifer. He was a local man and was not inexperienced with the law. Ronald had already served 18 months in prison for attempted sexual assault.

Cotton's history, of course, didn't help his case. During the trial, he was visibly nervous. He got his dates mixed up. His alibis didn't check out. A piece of foam was missing from his shoe, similar to a piece found at the crime scene. Circumstantial evidence was strong.

It was Jennifer Thompson's eyewitness account that sealed a life conviction for Ronald. He was found guilty and sentenced to life in prison. Jennifer had her justice.

Ronald, like all rapists, professed his innocence. His appeals were repeatedly denied. One day, a glimmer of hope surfaced for Ronald. Another woman had been raped just an hour after Thompson: same Burlington neighborhood, same kind of attack. Police were sure it was the same man. An appeals court had ruled that evidence relating to the second victim should have been allowed in the first trial. Ronald would get his second chance. Surely if the police believed that the rapes were connected and if he could prove he didn't commit that one, it would exonerate him from Jennifer's rape.

At the new trial, the witnesses would get a look at a second suspect, Bobby Poole, who was subpoenaed by Cotton's lawyer. Jennifer's convicted rapist had a second chance at freedom.

At the new trial, Jennifer's memories were brought to bear. Back on the stand, she was as confident as ever. She looked directly at the new suspect, Poole and she looked directly at Cotton.

Cotton is the man who raped me, she told the jury.

She was 100% certain of it.

The second jury was, too. Cotton hung his head. He had no words left inside him. Ronald stared in utter disbelief as the court handed down its verdict. His slim chance at freedom had just earned him a second term of life in prison.

11 years later, Jennifer Thompson had started a new life. She had a family a career and the flashbacks of the rape and trial were fading into the two dimensional, black and white memories of her past.

When Detective Gauldin knocked on her Winston-Salem home, Jennifer's faded memories were about to explode to the surface again...The detective hadn't just dropped by to say hello.

To finish the story go to www.bexsi.com/3 now.

Section III

~ Interaction ~

"We don't accomplish anything in this world alone ... and whatever happens is the result of the whole tapestry of one's life and all the weavings of individual threads from one to another that creates something."

~Sandra Day O'Connor
Supreme Court Justice

Chapter **Eight**

• • •

"All successful people began their journey by being unsuccessful at first."

~ Brian Tracy

• • •

Knowledge

What is knowledge? Sometimes we confuse the words information, knowledge and wisdom. In the pursuit of a worthwhile goal, one of your tasks is to become more knowledgeable in the pursuit of your goal. Acquiring the correct information will yield you knowledge and the consistent application of that knowledge will create wisdom.

If you have been in your present career for a decade or longer, are you more knowledgeable than the person who's just starting out in your field? Unless it's your first year, you know more than most of the people around you in your chosen career or your chosen industry. But like all knowledge, if you don't use it, it's irrelevant.

Knowledge is NOT power. You can be the smartest person in the world but if you don't use that knowledge, nobody will know how smart you are. Your genius, like a famous piece of artwork in the basement, is wasted. In fact, NOT applying your knowledge or the misuse of your knowledge is cruel to the rest of us. You and the value you provide are not meant to be hoarded.

Sharing whatever abilities, experiences and knowledge you have is more or less required. Why not increase the life experience of those around you?

Becoming a super achiever will naturally create new ripples in the lives of other people. Previously, those ripples may have been random, disorganized and unfocused. With your new attitude, energy, enthusiasm and power, they can create an exponential explosion of good in the lives of thousands...or more.

Real success is not a victory by a lone person. True success affects the lives of others in a positive and permanent manner. The B.A.R. model will not only spiral up personally. The victories you create also fuel the flames of other people in your life. In fact, your success will also affect the lives of people whom you never meet.

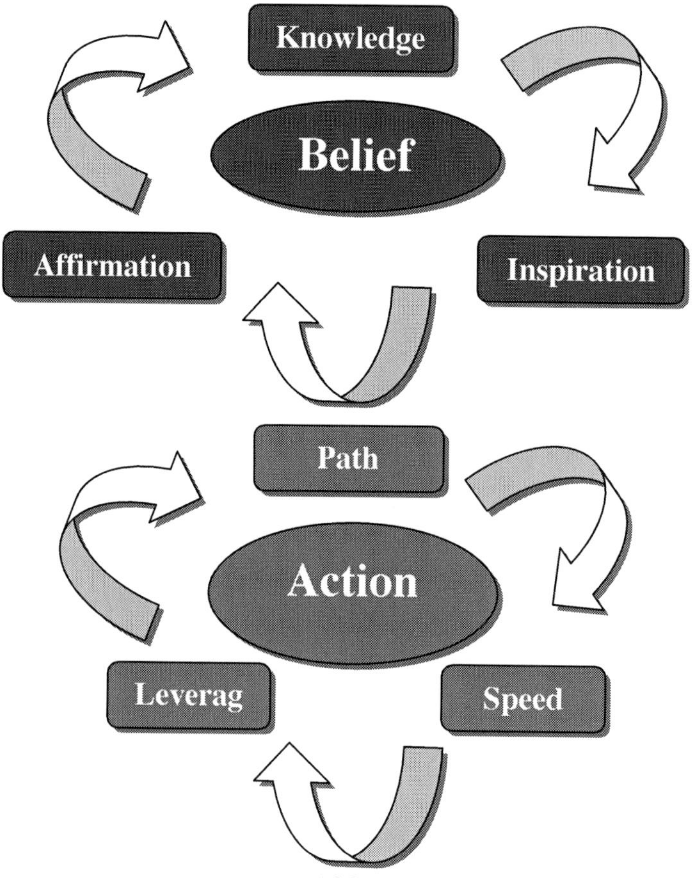

Knowledge

Acquiring the *correct* knowledge for what you want to achieve is an objective that sounds obvious to make. Unfortunately, rarely does an individual acquire the raw wisdom they need. Remember, your needs are NOT simply to attain a specific goal or objective, but establish a thought process, action plan and decision making system to cut out the clutter. Most people yield to the forces of marketing, the opinions of friends and the limiting self-beliefs of their past in their pursuit of knowledge. With these filters and influences, somebody else's agenda, instead of yours, is being addressed. Knowing and acquiring correct knowledge begins with understanding the differences.

Jack decided he wanted to start a part-time business. The idea of an extra $1,000, $2,000 or $5,000 monthly appealed to his sense of providing security for his family. He loved his career, but the ceiling on his time and income there had been reached. He wanted more.

He read business magazines, poured over business opportunities, franchises, network marketing companies and the infinite number of pitches of making money online. It was maddening.

One idea that caught his interest was vending machines. This was a part-time business that appealed to him because it didn't require him to sell the candy or sodas, they sold themselves. Pepsi and Coca Cola spent millions each month promoting their products and he liked the idea of being their partner. It was an all cash business. It didn't have any receivables or payables. He wouldn't need to do any billing; collections and his accounting would be exceedingly simple. With these foundational principles, he went off to do his core research. He was a college graduate, an accomplished business man, and it was time to make sure he understood where the potholes where, what challenges he would face, and what he potential was.

Jack called on 7 different providers of vending machines. He grilled the salesmen with questions about price, operation, placement and maintenance. He asked for references of satisfied customers and he called them up. He read reviews of different manufacturers and whenever he was out, he looked at other machines, what they were pricing their goods at and if they were full. Armed with a thorough investigation of the industry, the machines and business he ordered 8 vending machines at a total cost of about $12,000. At $200 per week in profit, he could expand his empire by rolling his profits into a new machine about every 8 weeks. Like any rational businessman, he figured within 3 years, he would have enough money rolling in to equal his full time income. His only job was to drive around to his locations one day per week, re-stock the supplies and pick up the loot.

He was excited.

Like 95% of all start ups, this one failed within 18 months. It wasn't a single event or missing piece of knowledge that doomed Jack's business, of courses. He did extensive research and rarely did he eat his own merchandise. The demise of his business was something that hindsight would have easily revealed the demise of this venture. Was it over-optimism? Was it unfiltered knowledge? Was it a mis-alignment of Jack's personality with this particular venture? In fact, it was the combination of over-optimism and filtered knowledge that doomed Jack's business from the day he started it.

Jack's failure was a result of filtered knowledge and mediocre associations.

• • •

"Associate yourself with people of good quality, for it is better to be alone than in bad company."

~ Booker T. Washington

• • •

Association

We tell our children to avoid hanging out with the "bad" crowd. A parent's focus on making sure their kids have responsible and respectable friends is important. As any parent will tell you, kids are malleable. They tend to become who they associate with.

"Don't hang out with that crowd," we tell our kids. "You'll end up on the wrong side of the tracks and in jail like your Uncle Ernie."

Yet, how often do you ask financial advice from a middle income stock broker, medical advice from an overweight doctor or relationship advice from a disgruntled divorced person. It is always easier to give our advice than to take it. Like the journalist's creed, "check your source" you will dramatically increase the quality of your future associations.

When you're out in the world, meeting people garnering information, transforming them into knowledge, not associating with losers may seem obvious. However, what about mediocrity? When you look for advice, support or information do you go to the very top international figure in your field? If you wanted to be in excellent physical condition would you emulate Jillian Michaels, trainer from the TV show, "The Biggest Loser" or a person of average physical condition? While it may be easier to relate to the average person, being average isn't much of a goal, is it? Being average doesn't actually work in the competitive environment we live and work it. Being average condemns you to lose in the battle between your positive self and negative self.

Local

Find the very best in everything you care about. In your search for knowledge to support your belief that you're going to get what you want and chose the goal that you're setting, your job is to find the number one person locally who has achieved that goal, who is a good example and has the right information for you. In the following pages, you will learn specific strategies for seeking out and associating with the top 1% achievers in your local area. Just as you encouraged your children to hang out with the right crowd, it is time to take your own advice.

Don't overlook the quality of the local talent around you. While you will pursue national and global source of knowledge, your local community will give you fast and local access while you are developing your "celebrity" rolodex of information in the coming months.

Global

Find the number one person in the world who has achieved a goal or lifestyle that you desire. Research candidates who have the supportive documentation, references and credibility to back up their fame. You may or may not be able to actually meet them, right away. However, you may find some national figures that you can not only emulate, but can use as coaches, counselors or mentors.

Since we are a social species, networking is a primary activity in our lives. I am not talking about social networking. There is a time and a place for social networking online. True networking with intent comes from reaching out and meeting the best of the best.

Filters

We all filter information. Our filters come in a variety of flavors. Your experiences, education and personality are all factors in how you digest and accept the information you receive. In the previous vending machine example, Jack was always optimistic. He always looked on the bright side of life. He was the poster child for optimism. While this characteristic is vital to success, it is a filter, nonetheless. To compound matters, the information he acquired was also filtered before HIS filters processed it! Calling on several different manufacturers is a good idea before plunking down $12,000 on a new business, of course. Any prudent investor looks at his options of course. However, when you are accepting and processing this information, instead of putting your filters on the data, it is better to understand THEIR filters first!

A salesmen's job is to sell. Every single piece of information he delivers to his prospect is designed to do only one thing...sell his product. That means that he is either attempting to build trust with his prospect or close the sale. Period. There is no other reason for him to invest any time with you. With that information your questions should be tailored to fit the anticipated response of what a salesman will tell you.

Ask for referrals? What do you suppose he will give you...bad ones? Of course they'll be glowing testimonials. But, when you call them, what questions can you ask in order to read between the lines?

What about reviews? Aren't people who critique companies, weight loss products and franchise opportunities there to give us unbiased opinions?

Unfortunately, there is no such thing as an unbiased opinion. Unless you are gleaning strict numerical data from a source, a reviewer or critic always puts their own personality, spin and opinion in their comments. As Jack Webb in the old TV series "Dragnet" used to blandly state, "Just the facts, ma'am" is a requirement when you are acquiring information and knowledge for your particular goal. Everyone has an opinion and is entitled to it. It is your job to know what their agenda is when dispensing that information to you. Perhaps it has never been as clearly stated as when the late president Ronald Reagan said, "Trust, but verify."

Acquiring the facts and opinions you need to make clear and correct decisions should not take a lifetime. Don't suffer from the paralysis of analysis. However, once you make the decision and ACT upon it, that doesn't preclude you from a steady dose of new knowledge and information.

The person who is at the top of their game, the number one in their field not only invests in the skills of their craft, but in the new, innovative and relevant knowledge that springs forth on a daily basis. A person who does well or achieves the pinnacle of success never earns the right to stay there without increasing their knowledge on a constant basis.

If you're not researching and getting information and transferring that information into knowledge on a consistent basis, day after day after day, you're going to get stale because the world changes. The economy changes, new technologies become available and new players are competing for your turf on a daily basis. The amount of information out there is overwhelming. Therefore, you're going to need a filter system to get the most relevant knowledge.

Using the internet WISELY is an important step. But you're going to need to set up some very specific filters to keep the junk out of your head because it's clogging up the system. With thousands of marketing messages bombarding our senses daily, you need to look for the premium sources of information for your interests, skills and goals.

“I am swamped already. I have ZERO time to start reading 3 newsletters per day, going to the library and reading a book every month. You don’t know how BUSY I am, Crowe!”

How do you eat an elephant?” the old joke begins.

“One bite at a time.”

Begin your journey to achievement with a single step. The Bexsi™ system is available to you. With an accountability platform to guarantee you succeed, you have nothing to lose and an incredible life to gain. Try it. You are invited to our social network as long as you make a decision to be successful in any endeavor where you have failed in the past.

www.bexsi.com and www.bexsi.org

Chapter **Nine**

• • •

"That which is feared, lessens by association."

~ Ovidius Naso
Ancient Roman poet and author

• • •

Goals without wisdom can be self-defeating or even dangerous.

"I'm going to lose 20 pounds by eating less sugar and working out half an hour a day."

Hey, that's great. Why? Do you know what it does to your body? Do you know about your body's insulin pump? Do you know understand what a hypoglycemic index is? Do you know what you're BMI is? Knowing all those things is not like learning how the solenoid works in a car. But what might be important for you, if your car breaks down.

So it is with your body, your mind, your attitude, your spirit, and your finances. The more you really understand the wisdom required to align yourself with the raw knowledge of your goal, the more likely you'll achieve it. Go ahead and enroll in school but make sure you balance your course work with generalized information, strategies, and wisdom along with tactical information and how to get things done for your specific goal, career or interests.

Read

Your job is to read one good book a month. Not a magazine. Not an article. Read one good book a month. If you can crank up that once a week, you'll be the top 1% of the achievers in the world. Go to the library. Do some research. Look at the books in our glossary and apply them. I know that many of us enjoy reading novels from time to time. This can be great entertainment and some classic works increase our vocabulary and education. Some classics were required reading in school. There is no law that says you can't read them later in life. A healthy combination of reading the classics and good books on wisdom strategy and life will make you a better person. Commit to reading one great book each and every month. It will make you more well-rounded, educated and interesting.

School

There are some schools out there that teach very specific things. Getting your degree or your masters in a particular subject has been popular for hundreds of years. It's less popular today because the economy and the marketplace changes so rapidly. By the time you graduate with many degrees, the entire industry where your degree is applicable has changed. General knowledge is not such a bad thing to do especially when it comes to getting wisdom. If you're working at a degree or you're still in high school looking for advanced degree, don't forget to interlace your specific course of study with the generalized knowledge. Learning *how* to think and absorbing wisdom takes time but it's time well invested because when you obtain that core knowledge and winning strategies, you can apply them to every area of your life.

Don't confuse wisdom, strategy and tactics. Each has its place in your drive to succeed. The reference section of this book categorizes which books fall under which category. School is a vital component of knowledge. Like books it is a time-tested method for learning. However, the most relevant classroom is the classroom of life.

Life

Perhaps the most expensive area of knowledge, is experience. Life is a great school. Along with reading this book and using a system right now, you'll be using the game of life to learn and achieve. Like most people who have large goals you'll be taking years and spending hundreds of thousands of dollars striving towards that goal. Previously you may have wondered why, year after year, you are moving so slowly, if at all, towards your goal.

Your excuses end the moment you opened up the first page of this book.

Getting the right knowledge means investing your valuable time with highly targeted information sources. One of my favorite authors and master networker, Bob Burg knows how to associate with the best. Be sure to read Endless Referrals. In any business or endeavor, who you know can be more important that what you know.

One area where networking can pay huge dividends is at your local chamber of commerce. Unfortunately, nearly everyone does it wrong...except you.

Chamber of Commerce

The most important network to start with is the one in your own backyard. Starting locally is very important, easy and inexpensive. Regardless of your endeavor, profession or goal; join the Chamber of Commerce.

Joining the chamber of commerce is easy. Maximizing your time there requires focused thought, efficient use of your time and decidedly giving spirit. Here are some guidelines that will make you the leader, give you unlimited resources and increase your value in any goal you have.

Be the hub of the wheel. If you have ever attended a chamber event, you'll notice that there are always a few key people who seem to know everyone. Often this is the chamber president, a long-term member and/or a person who is known for giving great advice, leads and business to others. This person is the hub of the wheel. Everyone knows him/her and he knows everyone.

Your job is to gravitate to this person and learn how to become them. This is easier than it sounds. When you attend a meeting and chat with someone, the odds are that 3 out of 4 times, you won't be a good prospect for them. People LOVE to talk about their business and how much value they can add to yours. Rarely does "Mr. Chatty" ask about how qualified you are to use their services. That's OK. Your job will be to listen and take good mental notes. Get their card and pay attention. They will become a cornerstone of the foundation you will be building.

Keep that person in mind and as you meet other people, you will discover than one of these new people are great prospects for Mr. Chatty. Introduce a qualified lead to Mr. Chatty and you instantly become the hub of a very small, but fresh and new circle of influence. You have become the hub of the wheel.

Send Thank You notes. The long lost art of actually sending a thank you note is in danger of becoming as popular as 8 track tapes. Thanks to email, text messaging and our frantic pace to focus on ourselves, people just don't take the time to send out a thank you note. In fact, there is a new network marketing business called, "Send Out Cards" which automates the process and makes it quick, simple and personal to accomplish this task.

When was the last time you received a hand written note from someone? Chances are, IF you received one, it caught your attention. This is because it is such a rare event, a personalized; hand written note stands out from the crowd of marketing garbage that hits your inbox or desk daily.

In fact, many would be networkers still think that sending a brochure or including a business card in their notes is networking.

It isn't. At the very best it is simply marketing. Don't do it. The purpose of networking is NOT marketing! The purpose of networking is to develop new relationships with people who know you, like you and trust you-PERIOD. Nowhere in that sentence do you see any reference to your business, marketing, sales or any message about what you do or why.

Your mission isn't to promote your products or service. Your 100% focus is to be known as the hub of a wheel for information, trust and business. Don't worry about your job, company or sales. That will naturally come later. In fact, it will come in a flood if you are patient and don't ask for it.

Join a committee. This is not something the average person does, of course. However, in exchange for a few hours per month of meetings, you are instantly elevated to the status of a leader. This is where you must be if you want to associate with other leaders and acquire the knowledge you desire. Staying in the trenches keeps you sifting through mountains of dirt to find the gold.

By volunteering to belong to or even lead a committee, you will rise to the requirements involved. You will be asked to do more, think more and lead a small group of people. If you are already a manager or supervise people at your job, this should be second nature to you. If you are not responsible for others at work, being a committee leader at your chamber of commerce will be a great addition to your resume. True leaders never shy away from leadership roles. Go for it. Become a committee leader and you'll belong to an inner circle of wealth, knowledge and success.

Give leads to others. Being active in the chamber means you are there to give and get leads for business. Like a fireplace that gives off heat, you expect to get something out of this membership. You want a tangible or at the very least, an intangible benefit to your business and/or your personal life. Like a fireplace, however, you need to give heat in order to get it back. What spark are you going to deliver? What tinder can you apply to fan the flames of success in your life?

By giving leads to others your reputation as a leader is sealed. I have belonged to over a dozen lead groups and networking organizations in my lifetime and I can instantly spot the true leaders; not by their stature at the meetings, but by the leads they GIVE to others. Be a giver. You'll reap the rewards in due course.

Expect nothing in return. Expecting a return on your investment of time and money is normal. Expecting it quickly is not. Don't expect to get a single lead, sale or scrap of information for your efforts quickly. Think of networking as old fashioned dating (not modern dating...I have no experience in that!). In dating the old fashioned way, you meet someone and over TIME you learn about them, share common interests and slowly let them into your heart. Trust and companionship come over time and is tested on a continuous basis. You don't EXPECT to marry the person after the first date and you shouldn't expect any huge return on your affections after a first or second date. (Like I said, the example is OLD FASHIONED dating!)

Business networking is no different. People are rightfully cautious about who they do business with. Changing vendors is not a process as painful or messy as divorce, but it does come with an appropriate amount of time. If you have an auto mechanic that you know, like and trust, why would you switch? By not EXPECTING to get any tangible business or intangible benefits from you efforts at the chamber, you accomplish a few things.

You put the people you speak with at ease. By talking about THEIR business, THEIR interests and THEIR needs, you have hit on THEIR favorite topic...themselves!

By not expecting anything in return, when the time is right for them (i.e. their comfort with you is sufficient) they will feel extremely obligated to give you knowledge, leads and business. You've deposited a fair amount of good will in their gas tank, eventually they are going to put their foot on the gas and get into your express lane to success.

The more you apply yourself locally, the more pure knowledge you will glean from proven winners in your neighborhood. Don't overlook this valuable and inexpensive resource to get the knowledge you need.

Associations

Join an association in your industry or an industry in which you are striving to excel in. You might not want to be a nutritionist, but what if you join the National Association of Nutritionists to get information for the next 12 months and to take that raw knowledge and apply it towards your own weight loss goals. Would you not become the poster child for healthy lifestyle, weight loss and nutrition, if you were part of the National Association of Nutritionists for at least a year? If your goal is a health goal, go ahead and act healthy.

Expect to become healthier and while you learn about health.

Get the right information from the right sources and apply it to your underlying foundation of knowledge. The application of that knowledge is true power.

Internet

The last area of knowledge will be the information you will find online. Your attention should be on how to best filter out advertisements and garbage. The best way to do this, whether it is an article, a website, an email, a blog – is to always look at the author's agenda.

When you find an article or website that interests you or you think can support your quest for good information, your eyes will naturally gravitate to the headline. After that, you'll start reading whatever THEY want you to see.

Stop.

• • •

"Know the agenda of your information sources before you invest your valuable time absorbing their content."

~ Doug Crowe

• • •

Go to the author's biography. Go to their About Us page and before you spend any of your precious time reading the next paragraph on their website, discern what their agenda is. Is the site or article opinion? Is it selling something? What is it? Just because they are selling something that does not mean it has less value than an industry review or the raw data from a government study. It simply means that their agenda will influence the content. You job is to know their agenda BEFORE you waste your valuable time ingesting their content.

Does that mean that if they are selling something, it's going to be tainted? Yes. Does that mean it is going to be incorrect? No. That's where your judgment comes into play. After you do that, you say, "I like what they are saying. I am going to check them out. Oh, they are selling a book on weight loss. Oh, they are selling a book on money." So long as you know their agenda, your BS glasses are clean and you can take and absorb what is valuable to you and discard what you don't find valuable.

Get references. Before you read the second paragraph, get references. Why waste your time? Why absorb information, which has a likelihood of being tainted. That makes no sense. That's worse than watching American Idol. At least American Idol has some entertainment value. But imagine putting the wrong information in your head and not finding out to a week or month or a year later that it was incorrect. The more proficient you become at this method of research and analysis, the better your information is and the higher quality your knowledge will become.

Consider how this process would have prevented mistakes in your past or at the very least saved you a considerable amount of your valuable time.

Step 1 – search online.
Step 2 – read one paragraph.
Step 3 – check out their agenda.
Step 4 – get references.

That is the key to saving your valuable time online. Do it every week. If you're an internet junkie, do it every day.

But do not spend so much time online that you chose not to make the time to meet people in person.

Here's why.

Let's say for example you received 30 emails today and assuming that you respond to five of them, the 25 you put in the later folder or re filed them. I will bet you the price of this book that 3 or 5 of those emails or all 5 were people that whom that you have **<u>already met.</u>** At the very least, the emails you opened, read and engaged with were from people you had a PRIOR relationship with.

This proves my point about the internet versus networking. It's great to market online. It's fantastic to have a social network to plug into online. But meeting somebody face to face, shaking their hand, looking in their eye, having a conversation with them, not a text conversation, puts them at the top of your mind. There are people out there who want to help you locally, regionally, and nationally. You ought to meet them.

Tim Ferriss, bestselling author of "The 4 Hour Workweek," is a self-proclaimed vagabond. He had a thriving Internet business and burned out. He simply left one day. When he "escaped" the rat race he didn't close his business down...he just left.

After a month, the business was still thriving (only the irritating customers left!) He focused on outsourcing EVERYTHING and was encouraged to write a book about it.

In order to promote his book, Tim didn't network ordinarily (chamber meetings, cruise the internet, etc.) He went to the VERY top. He found out where Mark Victor Hansen, of "Chicken Soup for the Soul" would be speaking and basically stalked him. He was able to get his attention for 30 seconds, pitched him the book idea and did it.

Most people network by happenstance or convenience. Rare is the person that seeks out and actually has the gumption to approach "celebrities" or people at the very top of their game. We are intimidated by their stature. However there is a specific technique and attitude you can take when approaching celebrities or powerful people.

Tim outlines this conversation in his book; I added a few nuances that I have found effective.

1. Call at least one potential superstar mentor every day for 3 days. Email them only after attempting these phone calls. Try calling at odd hours like before 8:30 or after 5:00 PM to reduce gatekeeper interference. Have a single question in mind...one that you've researched and cannot find online and that requires some thought and intelligence. Aim for "A" players, CEO's, Professional Athletes, Celebrities, Politicians, Famous Authors, etc.

2. DO NOT AIM LOW! People are people and you know that you will strike out more than get a home run, but ONLY if you swing multiple times. The higher you aim, the more likely your plans and goals will become reality quickly and with fewer derailments. If you are really shy and have some cash, use www.contactanycelebrity.com and use the following script:

"Hi, this is Doug Crowe calling for John Maxwell, please"

(answerer) "May I ask what this is regarding?"

"Sure. I know this might sound a bit odd, but I am a first time author and just read John's interview in the Reader's Digest. I'm a longtime fan and have finally built up the courage to call him for one specific piece of advice. It wouldn't take more than two minutes of his time. Is there any way you can help me get through to him? I really appreciate whatever you can do."

(Answerer) "I will give him the message" or "Hmmm....let me see. Just a second."

"John Maxwell here."

"Hi, Mr. Maxwell, my name is Doug Crowe. I know this might sound a bit odd, but I'm a first time author and a longtime fan. I just read your review in Reader's Digest and finally built up the courage to call. I have wanted to ask you a question for a specific piece of advice for a long time, and it shouldn't take more than two minutes. May I?"

"Sure."

(Insert intelligent question here) Thank you very much for being so generous with your time. If I have the occasional tough question-VERY occasional- is there a chance I could keep in touch via a short email?"

The words we use are VERY powerful. Casual confidence is mandatory. Too casual and they'll know it's fake. Too formal and you sound like a sales person. Saying "It's a bit odd" softens the person's curiosity. By introducing yourself promptly and properly you are answering their internal questions immediately "who is this and why are you calling me." Saying phrases like, "built up the courage" will also work wonders to melt any hesitation or barriers on their part. Of course, it may also explain the crack in your voice.

Now, when you go to meet somebody and you make an attempt to reach out to a high profile person, you probably won't get a return phone call right away. You might not get a return email. You might not get the social proof you need to validate the information or knowledge you are trying to acquire from this person. Which bring us to a critical attribute that all super successful people possess. Without this characteristic, all the knowledge in the world won't help you. Without a strong will to persevere, the agendas of others, your own negative self talk and an unclear vision will win and you'll lose another year in your quest to succeed.

Confidence

I heard an interview a few years ago about successful CEOs and business people, a lot of them visionaries. Companies that grow into the hundreds of millions of dollars all start with a single thought-a single person. Even multi-national conglomerates at one time or another, all began with the thought, vision and confidence from their founder.

Interestingly, a common theme among all of the CEO's interviewed was their unshakable confidence. Much of their confidence was in their idea, the market, and their team. The largest amount of confidence, however, was self-confidence. They knew, without question, that they could create something unique. When asked about that confidence, even when facing insurmountable challenges, they acted as if the future had already arrived. In fact, confidence in the future they envisioned, is what carried the company forward even after many had departed.

Many of these CEO's started their enterprises on a shoestring. They had no money, no backup, no team, and some had little experience. The one quality they all shared however was confidence in themselves.

In order to achieve YOUR plan, you will develop unshakeable confidence. Don't worry if you don't have it now.

Most people don't in the beginning. Through the systematic application of the fundamentals of this book and the Bexsi[tm] system, you will be given hundreds of rounds of ammunition. Your arsenal of examples, affirmations, visualizations and motivators will bombard your senses constantly. You'll also be getting daily doses of confidence from your own self-talk, from your mentor and from me. You have greatness within you.

You Are Great

God doesn't make any junk and you don't qualify for failure. The design of all species is to survive and thrive. As the most developed organism on the planet, humans have the most potential of all. We created societies, harnessed the atom and changed the very nature of a planet. We are incredibly imaginative, powerful and our ability to understand ourselves is dwarfed only by the infinite. Everyone is not born equally. We are not all born with a supportive parent or in a disease free environment. However, the opportunities for greatness are within us all. Skeptics may say, "Oh, how can *everybody* be great, Doug?"

Everybody is great. Some people, like Beethoven, discover their talents early in life. Colonel Sanders, of Kentucky Fried Chicken fame, did not harness his greatness until much later in life (He STARTED offering franchises at age 65 using $105 from his first social security check).

No matter whom you are or what you have or don't have, you have qualities that can be pulled out, exercised, strengthened and improved. Look at Stephen Hawking. From the age of 21 his paralyzed body became weakened by motor neuron disease to the point here constructing a single sentence with a voice synthesizer can take unbearable amounts of time.

Many people who are paralyzed and unable to communicate give up and die. Not Hawking. After Albert Einstein, he is perhaps the most influential physicist in history. Does this mean to be great you have to understand the inner workings of a black hole or be the CEO of a successful start up?

Of course not.

You can be a terrific parent. You can be the best son or daughter in the world. Being great can come in the form of anything that is important to you. In the eyes of a teacher, student, pastor or bystander, you can be a pivotal point for someone else. A single word, a comment or a slap on the back has the power to change the direction of another person. Who knows where the encouragement you give some else will go?

Who you are becoming? If your life isn't a journey, if it's not a positive experience on a daily basis, what are you doing? Why bother? Why are you here? Take up space? Watch American Idol? Why don't you do something? Why don't you change the lives of yourself, your family and your community? Why don't you go ahead and cure cancer?

It is important and even essential for you to have a positive attitude – to believe in yourself. Equally important to harnessing and directing your attitude is the confidence you must develop and share with others. This will help you in destroying negativity that others bring towards you. Deflect it and ignore it. You know that you are successful – you know that you are powerful. Don't ever let anyone take that away from you.

What would have happened if some people didn't ignore the negative comments of others? The very course of history would be radically different. For example:

- A music teacher told Beethoven that he was hopeless as a composer.
- Thomas Edison's teacher said he was too stupid to ever learn anything.
- Winston Churchill failed the 6th grade.

- A newspaper fired Walt Disney for having a lack of imagination.
- Michael Jordan was cut from his high school basketball team.
- Chicken Soup for the Soul was rejected 140 times before it was published.

What do all these people have in common? They all had massive and seemingly CREDIBLE negative input yet still believed enough in themselves to go on to not only prove them wrong but to be hugely successful and even change the course of history. There are countless stories like this from the famous, infamous and unknown. Encourage everyone.

"Oh, but I am not as smart as Thomas Edison," I hear you say. Really? Remember, EVERYONE is good at something. EVERYONE has value and worth beyond what they are doing right now.

Are you seriously thinking that you have ZERO untapped potential? Can you look yourself in the mirror and say that you give 100% every day for your entire life?

Of course not.

Therefore, if there is untapped potential in you, who knows WHAT you are capable of? Do you?

Your mind is the engine for all success.

All great things come from thought. Thought precedes action. Going after extreme success; however, requires more than a good expectation, a proper attitude and a firm belief in yourself being able to achieve it. What you also require is knowledge.

There are two thoughts to your brain. On one hand, there's your thought process, the attitude, belief, expectations. On the other hand there's the raw information of knowledge. "Yes, I believe I can go to the moon" but, "Gosh, I don't know how to do it".

Like a stick of dynamite, your potential energy is sitting there, waiting for you to light the fuse. The potential within you is infinite. Prior to any achievement, great or small, the potential lays dormant.

From an action as simple as planting a garden or as complex as putting a man on the moon, all activity and results begin with a single thought.

Your greatness is locked inside of you.

You have in your hands, the key to unlock it and release its full energy into the world. The power inside your mind and the actions and interactions you take will shape your world.

Take one single step today to lighting your fuse and creating an explosion of success. Visit www.bexsi.com now and start your mission to succeed.

Chapter Ten

• • •

"The quality of a person's life is in direct proportion to their commitment to excellence, regardless of their chosen field of endeavor."

~ Vince Lombardi

• • •

In the previous chapters much effort was placed on re-wiring your brain for success and creating actionable items to construct the life you want and reach for the potential you have inside yourself.

An increase in the **quality** of your actions will create better results for your life. How you act will determine the quality of your actions. Consistent effort will yield a different and better result than inconsistent action. Persevering in the face of obstacles will bend or break those obstacles to your will. Developing and listening to your intuition will yield efficiencies of speed by ten-fold.

You can walk or run towards your goals. While either speed will get you there, there are distinct advantages to going faster. Like perseverance, the degree to which you apply consistency and patience to your thoughts and actions will determine the quality of your journey and the fruits of your labor.

• • •

"Strive for consistency, don't worry about the numbers. If you dwell on statistics you get shortsighted, aim for consistency and the numbers will be there at the end."

~ Tom Seaver

Consistency

Without consistency of thought both conscious and subconscious you will waffle between ideas and action. Without consistent effort and action, no permanent change of habits and lifestyle will occur. Be consistent in all that you do, think, imagine and share. Imagine an athlete committing to a goal to run a marathon. If that runner had no experience in this area, he/she would have to begin training early on and CONSISTENTLY train.

You wouldn't expect them to work hard for 3 weeks, take off for 3 weeks, and be able to start up again where he left off. So it is with any goal whether it is financial, social, spiritual, emotional, or personal. Consistent effort is more important than making large, big strides. Remember the story of the tortoise and the hare. We are taught that fable at an early age. We may be teaching it to our children right now.

The best way to teach any subject is through example. Set a good example for others. Be a tortoise. Consistently and patiently move your goals forward by taking action-any action, on a consistent, steady basis. You may feel like you are moving at a snail's pace. The lack of results may be frustrating, but the reward at the end of the race will be phenomenal and totally satisfying.

If you TRULY want to supercharge your goal, then share it. If you really want to make your dreams a reality, then commit to your plan, and let someone else know about it. By being accountable to another person, you are laying it on the line. You have now put your very word at risk. Do not take this lightly.

More importantly, you must select an individual who will not let you off the hook! Share your goals, your action plan and your obstacles with someone who will hold your feet to the fire. Make sure they understand that the achievement of this goal is important to you.

In fact, if a person with the right personality is also one who may benefit from your goal (such as a family member) than so much the better. Just be sure you leave your emotional baggage behind you. If a friend holds you accountable to achieving a financial goal; and it takes longer than you planned (almost always does) don't allow their doubt or disbelief to slow you down. It is alright to get frustrated with yourself. But, it is detrimental to beat yourself up so much that it affects your attitude and dilutes your spirit.

In order to achieve your goals be sure to utilize all of the strategies and tactics available to you.

- Become passionate about your future
- Be clear about your specific goals and purpose
- Include an honorable cause beyond yourself
- Dream big
- Assign achievement dates to all of your goals
- Address your obstacles BEFORE they occur.
- Design multiple strategies for overcoming your obstacles
- Affirm the achievement of your goals in the present tense
- Speak your success into existence
- Reward yourself in a small way, on every goal you achieve
- Be accountable to a supportive person

Your mind and your heart can be your biggest ally or your biggest detractor. Use all of your resources and skills to achieve any goal you can dream of. By dreaming big and applying yourself steadily, you will accomplish more than you are aware of right now.

Your lack of accountability is keeping you from reaching your goals. Accountability is the main focus of Express Lane to Success. This isn't just a book about achievement – about being successful or about becoming a new person. The interactive component of this book provides a serious accountability system can force you to succeed where you have failed in the past. You can have a new lifestyle, a new purpose, a new direction and a clearer destination for your life.

How you apply it and how much time you dedicate towards improvement need not be overwhelming. By applying some easy changes, you can actually spend LESS time on improving and more time on winning.

How much are you worth?

If you are an employee or a professional, this is an easy calculation to make. Take your annual income and divide it, not by the hours you work, but by the hours in a year. Your LIFE is how you spend your time. Just because you cannot work 24 hours a day doesn't mean those hours don't count.

If you're at death's door and the doctors said you got a year to live, how would you spend it? What kind of value would you place on that single year of your life? Well, guess what? Someday you ARE going to have one year left!

How much is a year of your life worth? Put a dollar figure on it. Whatever that is, break it out on a monthly basis. Break it out on a weekly basis. We all know that life is precious, so this is merely an exercise to associate a dollar figure with the time we waste. For arguments sake, suppose your life has a value of $10,000,000. Or if your self-esteem is really in the toilet, say it's a $1,000,000. If you had a year to live, that equals about $83,000 per month or approximately $2,766 a day. We won't count required sleep of about 8 hours and that leaves 16 hours of productive time or about $172 per hour.

Every hour you waste watching some stupid TV show, reading some dumb magazine, listening to some jerk at a water cooler it's costing you $172 or more if you place a higher value on your life.

Life, of course is priceless. Another way to look at it is if you had the ability to generate income on an hourly basis of $100 or even $25, every hour you spend on activities that don't relate to your most important goal or objective is money, energy and time that is lost forever.

You can always make more money. Listen, I've earned millions and I've lost millions. I know what it feels like. It doesn't feel good, but what's worse was losing time because I can never get that back and neither can you. Your life experience is a critical component of your education. Value your time. Your life is made up of the stuff.

54 Weeks a Year

When it comes to pulling information versus having information pushed upon you, by following even half of the following time saving tactics, you can easily create an additional 1-2 hours per DAY of free time. I know of single working moms with 2 jobs who still create time to read thirty minutes per day and create a schedule that allows for 15 minutes of mediation and 45 minutes of exercise. The old saying, "If you want to get something done, give it to a busy person" isn't just a saying, it is a fact.

What would YOU do with an additional one week a year? How about 2 weeks? If a typical work day consists of an 8 hour day, I can give you a plan to create an additional 44 days or a FREE MONTH and a half of time each year!

How?

Stop watching American Idol, stop watching the news and stop clicking at every single ad that you see on the Internet. By simply applying a few of the following tactics, you can easily steal, shift and magically create an additional hour per day of fee time for yourself. That equates to 365 hours per year or over 44 eight hour days per year. You will have excuses, reasons and justifications on why the following ideas can never work for you. For just a few minutes, consider applying the following tactics and imagine your excuses or reasons didn't exist. You may work 60 hours per week, have a second job, 17 kids and a sick relative to take care of but we all have 168 hours per week. Nobody actually has more TIME than anyone else. We all have tasks, responsibilities and duties that we have CHOSEN!

"Oh no…you don't understand, my xxx works me to death!"

Sorry. You CHOSE that (insert job, spouse, hobby, excuse here) the only things you have not chosen for yourself are the biological requirements of survival (sleeping, eating and we'll also include adequate hygiene since we are a social species).

You chose your job or career.
You chose your spouse or partner.
You choose to have children.
You choose your entertainment.

You may not have chosen to be born and you didn't select your parents, but you CHOSE what you do with your time, every single day.

Here are 10 surefire time savers that are guaranteed to create an extra 1-2 hours per day of productive time. You can use this extra time for work, play or relaxation. The choice is up to you.

Email. Stop opening your email every hour. Remember when mail used to come once per day and you opened it when you got home? Our communication of email, texting and cellular communications had created a culture of immediate response. This is an EXPECTATION and not a requirement. You empower those who interrupt you. Let them know as tactfully as you can that you will be opening your email only once per day from now on and to expect a response within 24 hours if appropriate. You can train them to deal with YOUR schedule.

Multi-task. Don't multi-task when communicating with others. Focus your mind on one thing at a time. Multi-task only your mind and your body like reading your mail when taking a walk or listening to books on tape during a workout. When you multi-task your mind, you tend to switch between what you should be doing and what you shouldn't. By single tasking you are more likely to do what you are supposed to be doing. Typing a letter while you are on the phone doesn't save time. It irritates whomever you are speaking with and shows a lack of respect for their time.

Commute. Use commuting time as a university on wheels. Many people tend to zone out during their commutes. Driving the same route day after day, listening to music can be relaxing. So relaxing, in fact, that you don't even remember blowing through a stop sign! Use your CD player to listen to audio books on success, time management, weight control, or whatever interests you.

Paper. Touch paper one time. This is a classic time management technique. How many times have you shifted this pile from one corner to another? How many times have you kept old magazines, articles and newspaper clippings for use later? Use a 3 step filing system and adhere to it strictly. When you have any paper come across your desk either read it, file it for later or discard it. Period. That will declutter your desk, your mind and give you more time for what's important.

Magazines. Tear out magazine articles you are interested in and discard the rest. Unless you are in advertising or marketing, you don't need to read the ads or stories about Paris Hilton. Declutter your mind. Pull out ONLY the information that you want. Discard the rest. Compile a folder of these articles and set aside ONE time per week to look them over. After you are done. Throw them away. No…you won't need to read them again.

Big Tasks. Tackle your biggest tasks first. Read Brian Tracy's "Eat that Frog" and you'll learn that when you attack and focus on your biggest most important tasks first, you instantly have MORE time for the secondary, less important tasks. We tend to want to go after small things on our to-do lists because when we get a few small things done first, we feel like we are making progress. This small endorphin rush has been documented even when we cross off an item on our to-do list.

List. Make a priority list of all the things you want to do on a daily basis. Make a second list of your medium and long range goals. Put an "A" next to all the daily tasks that directly relate to your biggest most important role or long range goal. Do those first without exception. When you place a large percentage of your energy, time and thought on that big task, you'll get it done faster and better. Ask yourself the following question every day, "What task, if done in an excellent fashion, would have the BIGGEST impact on my life?" When you sincerely ask, answer and do that, you'll notice incredible time savings and immense satisfaction with your life.

Type. Learn to type properly. Our business culture dictates that we write correspondence, reports, essays, etc. almost daily. The faster you type, the more you get done and the more time you have. Your mind conceptualizes words, phrases and ideas at an amazing speed. Many executives dictate their ideas and have a stenographer transcribe it later. If you can afford a transcription service or assistant, you'll save countless hours. You can also use technology that simulates this service. Products such as Dragon Naturally Speaking work surprisingly well after you invest a small amount of time learning how to use them.

Read. Speed reading is similar to typing. Any decent speed reading system will increase your comprehension and by only tripling (A modest goal) your reading speed, you'll save huge chunks of time.

Television. By far, the biggest time waster on the planet is the idiot box in your living room. The average male 15 and over 'invests' 5.7 hours per week in leisure activities (5.1 hours for females!) with over half of this time being devoted to watching television according to the U.S Bureau of Labor Statistics. I know that finding out what happens to Jack Bauer this week is important. I mean, the fate of the country is in his hands and I may need to evacuate my family to...oh wait a minute. I forgot it is just a TV show!

In fact, our addiction to characters, plots and the endorphin rush we get with a story of romance, adventure or comedy can be addicting as any mild drug. Kicking the habit is difficult the first day or week. Trust me, you'll live. Kick the TV habit for 30 days and just see how much FREE time you actually have! It will shock you. With the increase time you create, you can start a business, lose 20 pounds effortlessly and you can always purchase the DVD set next year and watch it without those commercials! (Or digitally record it)

Take that initial 1-2 hours of time you create and go back and visit your local library? Huh? The library? Why go there instead of going online? The internet has its place, of course. Breaking news, technological advances and images are more rapidly accessed there. However, some of the best sources of strategy, tactics, and wisdom, have always been at the library. In the resource section of this book, you will find a collection of some excellent books on wisdom.

This wisdom will apply to everything. It will apply to your thoughts. It will apply to your attitudes, your belief and your expectations. This wisdom will insure you become a better person. It will make you a better parent, teacher, student. Wisdom can give you the foundation you need to lose those 20 pounds and it can create a philosophy of abundance that all multi-millionaires have.

Increasing your wisdom will naturally and effortlessly cause you to earn more money, live a healthier lifestyle and increase the quality of your interpersonal relations. You won't learn wisdom through a $29 weight loss program online or the newest exercise equipment you bought off of eBay. Your wisdom will come from the application of the sage advice of exceptional thinkers of the past.

Perseverance

Will, perseverance, drive, stamina, fortitude...these are the qualities of a winner. Do you have it?

If you expect to win and BELIEVE you will win, but don't stick to it long enough to realize the fruit of your labors, and you will have wasted a considerable amount of energy, money and time. Remember, time is all we have. Your time and how you invest it IS what your life is made up of. Would you knowingly end your life early? Most people wouldn't, but the amount of time wasted on "trying" or "attempting" a goal or objective and then quitting it is one of the biggest time wasters imaginable. It is the equivalent of a slow suicide.

When you harness the power of perseverance, all the time you invest in yourself and the pursuit of a fulfilling life is time well invested. Your journey becomes satisfying, rewarding and joyous. You begin to look forward to each day with expectancy. Your perseverance will be an attribute that literally saves your life.

On your road trip to success, you are going to have challenges. Any goal of any worth has obstacles. Of course, the larger the goal, the larger your obstacles ill be. This isn't an option. If your massive goal DIDN'T have massive challenges, it would be easy to accomplish by all and by its very nature, not be a large goal. It is a circular reference that is defeated before it can even begin.

Challenges are part of life. Imagine you rubbed the magic lamp, the genie came out and you had everything you wanted. You had all the money in the world. You had perfect health. You had perfect relationships. Everything is just delightful and you sat there in perfection like a lot of people who have had that kind of lifestyle. What would be the REAL result of such instant "success?"

There is evidence to support that getting without earning doesn't work. There are multitudes of stories about lottery winners who lose all of their winnings in a matter of a few years. Not having earned the money, they don't know how to manage it. Without the essential skills and experience of earning it, they cannot hope to know how to hold onto it and lose it all.

Similar declines of character, wealth and life occur with trust fund kids. Some are given all the advantages of wealth and prosperity and they still fall into a life of discontent. Having it "all" means little if you don't acquire the life skills necessary to apply yourself properly.

Classic examples of failure include young Hollywood celebrities or other children of billionaires who get hooked on drugs or lead lives of abundance without the effort required to earn it. When a person lives a life of reckless abandonment without responsibility, the results are nearly always the same. They don't truly have health, wealth and prosperity. Without wisdom, their fortunes work against them.

The roadway to success isn't paved with easy winnings and "luck" but the sweat and skills of determination acquired through overcoming the challenges along the way.

Perseverance is an undeniable quality of success. To persevere is to win. To persevere with knowledge, attitude and expectation and belief is to win **BIG**. To persevere with knowledge, attitude, belief, expectations, and speed is to win big faster than ever before.

Without perseverance, you can be knowledgeable but you won't win. Perseverance is the glue that will hold all of your other skills together.

As you develop a permanent positive attitude, your negative self talk will naturally diminish. As you increase the volume and clarity of your new self, your negative images of the past will shrink. When you filter out wasteful information and become the same type of leader than you seek, you'll become more successful at a more rapid pace. Along the way, your challenge will continue to assault these qualities.

Only perseverance will keep you on your Express Lane to Success. To maintain a positive attitude requires perseverance because you're going to get bombarded with negative attitude from yourself and others on a daily basis. To create the right belief in yourself and to affirm that belief takes perseverance because every day in every way, there are negative forces with contrary beliefs assaulting your brain. Perseverance is going to be as important as knowledge because you can't acquire top-level knowledge without persevering through the rejection and non-responsiveness of the high level knowledge that you seek.

Like thousands of successful athletes, Derek Redmond aspired to be an Olympic medal winner. The color of the medal was not important; his dream to stand on the podium and have just ANY medal grace his neck would be a dream come true.

He would earn his chance at the 1988 Games in Seoul. With years of training, encouragement from his friends and family and a hopeful nation watching, Derek was in prime shape. His years of preparation would be brought to bear in less than 10 minutes. His adrenaline was pumping furiously.

2 minutes before the competition, a hamstring injury shattered those dreams.

The following 12 months included eight surgeries, intense rehabilitation and advanced training. Derek's body was healing. He was young. There was another Olympic opportunity in just a few years. So when the 1992 Games arrived, he would be more prepared than ever to live his dream and to show the world an example of talent, patience and perseverance.

He was ready.

Derek's father, Jim was more than just a father. He was his biggest cheerleader and his best friend. Jim Redmond attended all of Derek's races. He never missed a single one and he would CERTAINLY not miss Derek's dash to an Olympic medal.

On the day of the race, Jim and Derek talk about what it took for Derek to get to this point. They remind each other of the pain, suffering, training, fortitude and determination Derek has. Derek has trained his body for years for this day. Pre-game time would be spent on mental preparation. No matter what, Derek was going to run the best race of his life. It was inevitable.

The semi-final heat would determine who would race for Olympic bronze, silver and gold. Of all the races Derek had run, this was the most important one of his career. It would be his best. His fastest. It would shape his destiny and put him in contention for Olympic medal. It would be the cornerstone of his career.

Even though it was a qualifying semi-final, the stands were packed with over 65,000 excited fans. The energy in the stadium buzzing, Derek lines up on the track. "This is it," he thinks. "This is the race of my life." He has never been more in tune with his body. He has prepared his entire life for less than 50 seconds.

He body is coiled like a spring, ready to let loose over 20 years of training, energy and hope. The gun fires. Derek breaks from the pack and quickly seizes the lead. He runs like a gazelle on speed. His mind is focused like a laser beam.

Halfway through the race, Derek is still pumping furiously. He doesn't look at the other runners. They don't exist. He is running for himself, his dad and his identity. Redmond is a shoo-in to make the finals.

With less than 175 meters left, Derek's hamstring snapped.

A snapped hamstring feels like getting shot in the leg. Derek's body responded in kind and collapsed onto the track. In a split second, two decades of a singular dream for Olympic gold was snatched from his life.

As Derek lies, bunched up on the track, clutching his right hamstring, a medical personnel unit runs toward him. Simultaneously, Jim Redmond, seeing his son in distress, gets on his feet and races down the stadium aisle. Being seated near the top where the Olympic torch burns brightly gave him comfort and hope for his son's success. The high vantage point also created an incredible distance between him and his son. He doesn't care. He races to the track.

As a medical team shows up with a stretcher, Redmond tells them, "No, there's no way I'm getting on that stretcher. I'm going to finish my race."

The other runners have finished the race when in a coordinated show of disbelief, all 65,000 people watch as Derek, in excruciating pain and about as agile as a one-legged person, manages to rise to his feet in front of the crowd of 65,000 fans.

Slowly, the crowd, in total amazement, rises and begins to roar. The roar gets louder and louder. As if the crowd could transfer by sheer will, enough energy to heal his leg, they shout, yell, applaud and weep for Derek. Through the searing pain, Derek reflects, "Whether people thought I was an idiot or a hero, I was going to finish that race."

One painful step at a time, each one shallower and more painful than the first, and his face twisted with pain and tears, Redmond staggers onward. The crowd goes bezerk.

Jim Redmond finally gets to the bottom of the stands, jumps over the railing, dashes past a security guard, and runs to his son, with security not far behind. "That's my son out there," he yells back to security, "and I'm going to help him."

Jim reaches his son about 120 meters from the finish line and holds him up.

"I'm here, son," Jim says softly, hugging his boy. "We'll finish together." Derek, favoring the destroyed leg, leans on his father, continues to hobble and sobs.

The stadium of 65,000, all on their feet continue their thunderous roar. A few steps from the finish line, Jim releases his support of his son. Derek crossed the finish line, crippled, in pain and in a crushing defeat, but he finishes. His perseverance is immeasurable. His father later told the press, "I'm prouder of him than I would have been if he had won the gold medal. It took a lot of guts for him to do what he did."

Derek Redmond did not win that race or achieve his dream of an Olympic medal, but he created an example of perseverance that will outlive us all.

http://www.youtube.com/watch?v=Nifq3Ke2Q30

In many ways, perseverance is contrary to not only human nature, but to nature itself. There are quitting tendencies in all of us. Brian Tracy talks about being lazy as being a quality. He doesn't call laziness as a negative or positive quality. Laziness is simply a quality. It is a fact that if I was giving you a choice between earning in million dollars in one year or 10 years, each and every one of you would select one year. If I were to say I will give you million dollars the easy way or the hard way, each and every one of you would select the easy way over the hard because we are naturally lazy. By their very nature, all things of value require more effort. (Otherwise they wouldn't be as valuable!)

It isn't good or bad, it just is. Why do something difficult if the option is there to do it easy. Perseverance is required because you can't do anything of value easily. Creating a valuable experience, attaining a worthwhile goal comes with effort; with extraordinary effort. If it didn't have extraordinary effort, it would not be a worthwhile goal. I used the Olympics as an example. If it was easy to run a 4-minute mile, everybody would be doing it and it wouldn't be great. So, the very nature of greatness; the very qualities of a worthwhile goal for yourself are going to require perseverance.

Perseverance applies towards everything in life. In fact, perseverance is a key element of survival. Growing up watching public television, I was captivated by the life and death struggles in nature. The leopard chases the gazelle. Most, but not all of the time, the gazelle wins and the leopard loses. Both creatures persevere for their literal survival.

Why do you persevere? Are you going to persevere for a reason, or just to persevere? Is your perseverance directly connected to your survival? If so, that's all the motivation you need, you're set on your goal, you don't need anything else.

The progress of our society has all but eliminated the likelihood of not surviving. Most likely, you are reading this to thrive, not truly survive. Sure, some of you have hit bottom, gone through bankruptcy, divorce, or financial ruin. But that is not TRUE survival. As long as you have food, shelter and clothing, you are technically surviving.

Treating your objective as though your life depended on it would be a great motivator, but it simply isn't practical. Your ability to persevere can be developed and improved through the inspiration of others and the achievements you will claim. If you can associate with the perseverance of a life or death struggle, no clearer is this example as in the case of human conflict and wars. There are tremendous stories of soldiers who persevere when they've run out of ammo, and they continue to fight hand to hand.

During the Battle of the Bulge in WWII the German forces surrounded a small town in Belgium, Bastogne. Bastogne was then held by the 101st Airborne Division and was located at a critical crossroads that could have let the German army get through to American lines. This would have led to the German army retaking the important port city of Antwerp.

The American troops were surrounded. They were running low on food and supplies and the cold weather was beginning to take its toll on the men. The situation looked bleak for the American forces. Winning was impossible and surrender seemed inevitable. The German forces sent a messenger to deliver a request to surrender to Brigadier General Anthony McAuliffe. The first response that McAuliffe had was "Us, surrender? Aw, Nuts!" He then pondered what his actual response should be. The American officers decided that the first response should be the one they used. So, they sent back the note to the Germans:

The note was given to a German soldier to deliver. The note was passed between several German soldiers. None of them could speak English well and did not know what the note meant. They had never heard the expression "Nuts". So, the Germans decided that it meant "Go to Hell".

To: The German Commander
From: The American Commander

Nuts!

The troops, without rest, food and almost out of ammunition, were able to hold off the German forces with one single word. The term "Nuts" went on to symbolize American determination to overcome adversity against all odds.

Those who don't persevere often quit out of desperation, anger or fear. Perseverance is a very important quality to whatever you're trying to succeed at. You're issue is going to be your desire and your passion to persevere because of that goal.

People quit for one reason, they quit because a goal wasn't that important to them.

You set a goal to earn a million dollars and you don't hit it, do you quit or do you set it again like I did – five, six years in a row. You set a goal to lose 20 pounds in 90 days. Ninety-one days, you've lost 2 pounds or gained five. Do you quit or do you persevere?

The answer lies within the benefit of your goal. Is your goal worthy of going after repeatedly? The larger your benefit, the more likely you'll achieve it. The bigger your reward, the more likely you won't quit. It makes perseverance actually easier for you if there is no option to quit. The Express Lane is a Success will work for you. Once you enroll, you have planted your flag in sand. You can't quit.

Perseverance gives you the energy to keep going but it accomplishes much more than that. There is a leveraged result that can catapult your success and make you impervious to criticism, defeat and discouragement.

As you're persevering, you're assaulted by outside and inside forces of your self talk, your belief, and your expectations.

What about the world?

What if the world rejects your goal and bombards you with "You can't do it. You have no money. You have no experience. This won't work." The more you persevere, the more likely you'll win because of your perseverance.

Nature bends to the will of those who persevere. Like a

● ● ●

"Success is given to the person who knows the pain of perseverance is less than the pain of failure."

~ Doug Crowe

● ● ●

tree that takes root in the wall of a cliff; perseverance will crack the rock wall and allow more roots to take hold. The longer you persevere, and the more you tell yourself and the universe that you're not going to quit, the faster the universe bends to your will.

Who will you touch by the achievement of your goal?

Your family, friends and work associates may reap huge benefits by your success. Even casual acquaintances you'll meet through our achievers network will persevere because of your story.

Someone will be inspired by your story. Someone will be motivated by your success. Someone will be empowered by your challenges and even by your temporary setbacks.

Even if you're goal isn't as noble as to find a cure for cancer, you're involvement with the system will change the world and touch the lives of someone who needs it. Even if only one person decides to act because of the inspiration of your story, it may be all that is required.

Speed & Patience

Perseverance and patience are inexorably intertwined. In fact, a subset of perseverance is patience. Olympic athletes, like Derek Remond, have the perseverance to train daily for years in exchange for a race that lasts less than a minute. In conjunction with that perseverance, an attitude of patience is essential. Without the patience to wait for your perseverance to come to fruition, the average person quits.

Regardless of the size of your goal, perseverance must be balanced with a patient heart. Your large goals should be broken down into small tasks, small objectives in order to combat an impatient attitude. Large goals are never achieved in a blink of an eye. Certainly, there's evolutionary concepts that evolve or spark in our brains in a flash. However, bringing them to fruition requires the perseverance of an Olympic athlete and the patience of a saint.

Because large goals require so much time, a lot of us lose the energy to persevere. We get impatient with ourselves. "I'm going to lose 20 pounds in 20 days." In those 20 days, you've lost one. "I'm going to keep going. Well, maybe. I don't know. Maybe it's not for me. Maybe I'm not supposed to be thin. I'm just big boned." That's why large goals have to be broken down into smaller objectives and manageable tasks. When you have patience, you have staying power.

Perseverance takes effort. It wears us out. It saps our energy. You have failed before because you quit. Your excuses took root and grew more powerful than your reasons. Ending this cycle requires a system to prevent that from happening. You need daily doses of motivation to keep you engaged. We all need reinforcement of our positive actions to increase our belief. Of course, we can become frustrated when no tangible progress is seen or felt. Therefore, we're going to assault all of your negative and self defeating thoughts and actions on a daily basis. You can renew that energy on a daily basis, through the tools available to you through our Bexsi[tm] network.

Creating an attitude of patience in the hectic world we live in is challenging. *Instant success*, *10-day weight loss formulas* and our microwave society often reward speed ahead of quality. For permanent success to take root, a patient heart is required. Using the untapped power of your subconscious is one simply method to leverage perseverance and patience.

Patience

Breakdown your large goals into manageable tasks and you will create milestones. Each of these milestones will give you a result.

In the bar model B-A-R model, we know the belief causes action, action causes results, and more results create reinforce more beliefs. With a small milestone of success comes a physical reaction in our bodies. The small endorphin rush of checking an item off of a 'to-do' list or losing those first 2 pounds affirms our confidence and achievement.

Patience is critical because when we break a large goal down to smaller tasks, we actually don't need as much patience! The patience required to wait a year can be broken down into the patience to wait a month for a milestone to be reached. For the extremely impatient person (I am one of them), break it down by the week or by the day. The patience required to wait a day for a small milestone is certainly easier than what is required to wait a year or longer for the ultimate payoff of your goal.

A goal to lose 20 pounds is not done 20 pounds at a time, right? You didn't pack that extra weight on all at once. You did it over time. If it took you three years to pack on 20 pounds, don't expect it to come off in three days.

That doesn't mean, of course, that it will take you three years to take it off, either. But you can do it in manageable tasks. Depending on what system you're using, it should be a physical combination of education, nutrition and exercise. Mentally it should contain positive expectations, attitude and beliefs.

With the combined strategy of action and thought, you will create a new habit that will become effortless.

For reducing excess weight, start with a small objective of shedding just two pounds a week. Every Friday at 7 a.m. you weigh yourself. Wow! There it is; I lost a pound. If there are no results in the first week, you won't quit, but doubt may creep in. Before you allow a shred of doubt to take root, take an honest look what you did, check in with your coach or mentor and either continue the same plan for the second week, or adjust as necessary.

Use feedback as a circuit breaker and either reset it and do the carry on as before, or make an adjustment.

Of course, there are two tracks of patience you must be aware of. You have the daily track of repeated action with no instant results. With a small weekly reward (Like that scale smiling up at you with a lower number) you create fuel in your mind and body to do it again.

This also is where danger lurks. With achievement comes the expectation of additional rewards. Maybe you celebrate with a bowl of ice cream, or a "day off" of your new lifestyle. By reverting to your old actions, you may not think it is damaging to a habit, but it can be fatal to your goal.

Something happened; you went out of town, there was a party or perhaps you went to a vacation. In the span of a few days, you gained back what you lost in a week.

Oops.

At this point, most people's negative self talk says, "Oh, this doesn't work." I'm going up and down on the scale. This isn't working for me. I'm going to quit. I am big boned. I've always had low metabolism. Blah, blah…

With patience, short term milestones and circuit breakers, you can accomplish anything. Patience is required. A combination of patience and perseverance will allow you to attain what you seek. Without it, your life will be a constant circle of frustration, hope and justification. Is this the life you want? Is this the example you plan on leaving behind?

Break it down and stick to it. Bexsi[tm] can hold you accountable. Get started.

Developing the perseverance of a winner doesn't come easy. Frustrations, setbacks, disappointments and temporary losses are part of life. The mission at Bexsi[tm] is to give you the right thoughts, clearer vision and measurable action to claim your victory.

Focusing on your core strengths, delegating tasks that you are weak at and bombarding your mind daily with the right words will create the internal strength you need to succeed.

Speed

Combining speed with patience is not incongruous. Speed of activity and speed of thought is different than speed of expectations.

Don't confuse speed of action with patience of expectations.

Your success is determined by all the factors that we outline in the book and system for you.

- **Decision:** Deciding to win is the first step
- **Clarity:** Having a clear goal is imperative
- **Attitude:** A positive attitude is essential to your success
- **Expectation:** Change cannot come without making room for success
- **Affirmation:** Instilling a new belief in yourself is critical
- **Knowledge:** Seeking the right knowledge and network will support you
- **Perseverance:** Without persistence, your obstacles will overwhelm you
- **Patience:** Patience of results increases with the size of your goal

The speed with which you apply those principles is critical to your success. The speed with which you decide will empower you. Consider the last time you made a decision and didn't give it a second thought. You trusted your gut instincts and you acted. Isn't that decision right most of the time? Some people call that intuition.

Of course we all have some degree of intuition. The dictionary describes intuition as the understanding of knowledge without apparent effort. Digging further, we have discovered that your intuition can actually be strengthened. Your "intuition muscle," like a physical muscle, can be exercised, conditioned and improved.

Think faster.

Act instantly.

Trust your intuition.

Imagine the possibilities if you could trust your intuition more readily. What would your life be like if you acted 10X faster and were right twice as often? Could you accomplish more? Would that increase your income?

Colonel John (Richard) Boyd was a United States Air Force colonel, fighter pilot and military strategist, whose theories have been highly influential in the military and in business. He developed the concept called the OODA loop.

OODA stands for Observe, Orient, Decide and Act. The concept was originally developed and applied to military combat operations. As a strategic concept it is also very useful when applied to other processes such as business operations. The OODA loop strategy creates a recurring cycle. This allows you to quickly process events – processing them much more quickly than the opponents. Once you get used to OODA loop strategy you can easily navigate through the steps without any real thought process. Consider a fighter pilot being scrambled to shoot down an enemy aircraft.

Before the enemy airplane is even within visual contact range, the pilot will consider any available information about the likely identity of the enemy pilot: his nationality, level of training, and cultural traditions that may come into play.

When the enemy aircraft comes into radar contact, more direct information about the speed, size, and maneuverability, of the enemy plane becomes available; unfolding circumstances take priority over radio chatter. A first decision is made based on the available information so far: the pilot decides to "get into the sun" above his opponent, and acts by applying control inputs to climb.

Observe: Is the attacker reacting to the change of altitude?
Orient: Is the enemy acting like a noncombatant?
Decide: I am going to add power and pull the stick back.
Act: Pull stick back, anticipate next move.

As the dogfight begins, little time is devoted to orienting unless some new information pertaining to the actual identity or intent of the attacker comes into play. Information cascades in real time, and the pilot does not have time to process it consciously; the pilot reacts as he is trained to, and conscious thought is directed to supervising the flow of action and reaction, continuously repeating the OODA cycle. Simultaneously, the opponent is going through the same cycle.

How does one interfere with an opponent's OODA cycle? One of John Boyd's primary insights in fighter combat was that it is vital to change speed and direction faster than the opponent. This is not necessarily a function of the plane's ability to maneuver, rather the pilot must think and act faster than the opponent can think and act. Getting "inside" the cycle — short-circuiting the opponent's thinking processes - produces opportunities for the opponent to react inappropriately.

Another tactical-level example can be found on the basketball court, where a player takes possession of the ball and must get past an opponent who is taller or faster. A straight dribble or pass is unlikely to succeed. Instead the player may engage in a rapid and elaborate series of body movements designed to befuddle the opponent and deny him the ability to take advantage of his superior size or speed. At a basic level of play, this may be merely a series of fakes, with the hope that the opponent will make a mistake or an opening will occur. But practice and mental focus may allow one to reduce the time scale, get inside the opponent's OODA loop, and take control of the situation - to cause the opponent to move in a particular way, and generate an advantage rather than merely reacting to an accident.

The same cycle operates over a longer timescale in a competitive business landscape, and the same logic applies.

Decision makers gather information (observe), form hypotheses about customer activity and the intentions of competitors (orient), make decisions, and act on them. The cycle is repeated continuously. The aggressive and conscious application of the process gives a business advantage over a competitor who is merely reacting to conditions as they occur, or has poor awareness of the situation.

In Boyd's OODA loop theory all the decisions that you make are made as a result of observation of the current situation. Of course each person views the situation differently because he or she is looking at the information from a unique perspective. Everyone brings his or her own background, culture and experiences with him – that is the Orientation in the OODA loop.

You must loop through the process continually. If you get stuck you won't complete the process. In a combat that could mean losing permanently. For military strategists, it truly is a life or death situation. The OODA loop is not an option; it becomes a strategy of survival.

If we apply Boyd's OODA loop strategy to civilian life it means that we can't allow ourselves to get stuck in any one spot. We must constantly and continually go through the steps – Observe, Orient, Decide and Act. The last segment, action, is necessary to keep the loop going. That is where many people fail to reach their goals. They may have good intentions, they may be able to observe, orient and decide, but without action the whole thing collapses. So it is with your goals.

When you use your intuition, you're usually right and you're usually right for a reason, it's because your first inclination comes from your heart. It comes from your subconscious. It comes from a combination of all those things. The moment you doubt yourself, you're inserting negative thoughts into your head.

Practicing speed of thought requires time. Some people think, "Oh no, I want to mull things over and digest it because the more I mull it over, I come with the right decision." You might do that. However, in the end when you're all done mulling it over, you'll find out that more often than not, your first instinct was correct. The difference is you wasted an extraordinary amount of time vacillating between two choices when your intuition knew INSTANTLY what the correct path was.

Should I eat just ONE cookie? You intuition says, "Of course not." There is not a need for discussion. But, the devil on your shoulder keeps nagging at you and bombards you with justifications, excuses and reasons why it is OK, even though your conscious mind, subconscious though and intuition all say. "No."

Do not confuse speed of thought with speed of expectations. The quicker you think and act delivers an advantage to your action process every single time. (Not to be confused with a patient expectation of results; which requires more time.)

If you look at life as a competition, be fast and be first, put your opponent off guard. The more you anticipate an act ahead of the other person's thoughts and actions, the more you win. If you're in a collaborative effort, the more you are in-tune and act quickly on things it gives you two things. When it comes to the dialogue in your mind...trust your gut. Your negative self (NS) is the competition. Observe your NS, orient to thwart its power, decide to act and take the action. By pre-empting your own NS thoughts and behaviors, you can win the battle between your negative doubt and positive expectation.

The benefits of trusting your intuition are countless. When you're right, it gives you more time to enjoy your successes, more time to spiral up the entire process on whatever you're deciding to do. And if you're wrong, and you've acted quickly and it was the wrong decision, which does happen, by doing it quickly, it gives you more time to fix it, correct it and do it again.

As with all the concepts you will refine in your Express Lane to Success, combining correct knowledge with your intuition will yield you the results you truly desire. And of course this may not apply if you're an airline pilot or an ER surgeon. Making a mistake there can cost lives.

I am a private pilot and enjoy general aviation. A few years ago I took my kids to summer camp in a little single-engine Piper Cherokee. I had spent the previous 18 years of my life reading about aviation, studying accidents, getting my pilot's license and practicing.

A popular pastime of mine is reading aviation journals. In many of these journals, there is a section regarding accidents and fatalities, which some of you may consider a morbid subject. However, that is precisely the reason our government spends millions of dollars investigating major airplane incidents and crashes; so we can correct mistakes of the past and not repeats them.

The recurring theme I saw in general aviation accidents in smaller planes was a person's lack of training and decision making process. The more I trained for emergencies, the better prepared I was for them. Preparing for the worst and expecting the best is a common theme.

On a clear summer's day over the Northern Illinois skies I would be putting my training to the test...a test that could have easily ended my life.

One of the most dangerous times of aviation is immediate take-off and the landing. In cruise flight at a high altitude, if anything goes wrong, you run out of gas or something fails; small planes generally glide very, very well. And good pilots can generally glide towards an airport or towards an open field and survive.

The most dangerous time for aviation is always when you're close to the ground which naturally occurs on every take-off or landing. Extra diligence, concentration and the bulk of flight training revolves around it.

I was on a short hop between my home airport at DuPage county Illinois and my kids' summer camp in Eastern Iowa. As I lift off and star my climb, at a mere 500 feet above the ground, the engine coughs once and I am greeted by the deadly sound of silence.

My engine quit.

When you read about these types of emergencies, people tend to panic when the noise outside and the propeller stops. Sometimes you have time to decide what to do and think things through. On take-off, with only 500 feet of altitude; you don't. There are hundreds of sad stories where pilots freeze or instinctively try to turn back to the airport. In most cases, with 500 feet of altitude or less, they don't make it.

Part of training is to have a checklist for emergencies. This list is conveniently located in the glove box. The procedure for restarting an engine on this particular aircraft was located on page 36 of a 220 page manual. It would require about 2-3 minutes to locate the appropriate procedure.

I had 3 seconds.

If I had even attempted to pull out the checklist, the time it took would have exceeded my time in the air. Game over. If I had tried to turn and glide back to the airport, my altitude was not sufficient to make the runway. Bad idea. Without pulling the checklist out my hands swept through the instruments without any conscious thought on my part. It was as if my hand had a mind of its own. I watched as my right hand glided over the three items to check when the engine quits; throttle, mixture and fuel.

Throttle-in full.
Mixture-rich.
Fuel-select fullest tank.

Oops.

I noticed that the fuel selector was set on the same tank I had used for my inbound flight to Iowa. This was the outbound flight and that tank was bone dry. I flipped to the other tank and the engine roared back to life.

My instant reaction to that emergency saved my life, and allows me to share my story about speed of thought. How the perfect combination of knowledge and intuition causes an OODA loop of action that literally saved my life.

Refining your intuition muscle will pay you dividends time and time again. Thinking quickly and acting in accordance with your intuition will serve your goal nicely. You may not save your life in an instant, but you can expect to create a life by trusting it more often.

To read more about honing your intuition, log on to www.bexsi.com. There are articles there that you will enjoy reading.

Chapter **Eleven**

• • •

"We cannot live for ourselves alone. Our lives are connected by a thousand invisible threads, and along these sympathetic fibers, our actions run as causes and return to us as results."

~Herman Melville

• • •

BUTTERFLY EFFECT

"I don't have any big dreams, Crowe. I am very happy with simply raising my family and being a good example." Isn't that enough? Do I have to cure the common cold or invent a better ball point pen to make a difference?

No.

Dreaming big doesn't require you to take over a country or invent the next internet. Dreaming big, achievement and success comes in a wide variety of flavors and options.

Janice Warren was a college graduate. She earned her MBA while working full time at a bank. Her life was on the fast track to success. Her dreams included making an impact on the banking industry in the Midwest. She was creating a reputation in Chicago and climbed the corporate ladder steadily, but not with ease. She worked long hours and patiently created value for her company.

Day after day she made the right decisions and impressed the right people. Year after year she received raises and either a promotion or changed companies. Her power, reputation and experience rose steadily.

Then she had her first baby.

Determined to balance family and work life, she did what most working moms do...everything. Her duties, not shared equally with her husband were not an inconvenience at first. She continued to work full time and had her child in day care. It wasn't an option to quit. She loved to work.

Then the second child came. Then a third.

By this time Janice had cut back her hours and was working part-time. Her aspirations for being a six-figure executive in the upper tiers of the banking industry were replaced with the innocent, hopeful eyes of three beautiful children. Her big dreams were being replaced with raising three children. Is that a big dream? Does that qualify for making the world a better place? Will Janice attract grant money and a team of professionals to raise her three kids with her?

No. Her previous dream is gone. Her new mission is to simply be known as being a good mom and raising three happy and productive children. It may not sound as flashy as creating a multi-million dollar company or starting an orphanage, but it suited Janice just fine. She felt as though it was a worthy goal, nonetheless.

Janice was about to discover that nothing could be further from the truth. Her "small goal" of raising three happy children may result in saving the lives of over 100,000 people and inspiring a nation.

That story is still being written.

• • •

"You may achieve great things, but you haven't completed the circle of success until you help someone else move to a higher ground and get to a better place."

~ Oprah Winfrey

• • •

Janice never heard of the butterfly effect, but she was embarking on it nonetheless. She won't be building a corporate empire or curing cancer, but her dream to raise three exceptional children have the potential to do those things and more...much more.

Several years ago author and speaker Andy Andrews was working with the US Air Force and was tasked with finding the "proof of the value of an individual life". This was in response to a concern in the growing numbers of suicide within the armed forces.

The answer seemed so simple yet so complex. It seemed an impossible task – determine the measure of a man's life. Andy dug into the concept in earnest. He stumbled upon a theory called, "The Butterfly Effect" a doctoral thesis that was written by Edward Lorenz in 1963. The theory states that the infinitesimal movement of a butterfly's wings in Asia could cause a hurricane in North America. As the butterfly flaps its wings, tiny molecules of air are disturbed. Those molecules affect others and so on. These air molecules set in motion affect air movement until eventually the entire weather pattern on the other side of the world has been influenced. The theory, however, was laughed off at the time as ridiculous.

By the mid 1990's nobody was laughing.

A group of physicists proved that Lorenz hypothesis as fact. People working independently across the globe authenticated the thesis. The thesis is now commonly called "The Butterfly Effect" and is documented as a law of physics. The Butterfly Effect is considered to be part of the broader evolution of chaos theory named the *Law of Sensitive Dependence Upon Initial Conditions*. I think "The Butterfly Effect" is easier to remember.

There are an infinite number of stories that prove the Butterfly Effect to be true. In your lifetime you may or may not see a hurricane created from the small differences you make in the world. You may not see the millions of lives saved by your great-grandchild's success at curing cancer or developing a new process for growing food. However, the actions you take *will* have an effect on the world.

This book is dedicated to Juan Ramirez That is probably not a name that many people know. When Juan was 15, he crossed over the border from Mexico to Texas and was beat up and returned. As a juvenile, this was a vivid and frightening experience.

Juan did it twice.

On the second crossing he was determined to make a difference in the world. Even though he did not finish high school, he was committed to getting his GED and passing the exam to become a citizen of the United States. Working 2 jobs and supporting his young family, he barely had time to sleep, let alone study. As a 28 year old man, Juan's English was that of a 4th grader in the USA.

I owned an apartment complex many years ago and Juan was a tenant of mine. Despite his humble beginnings and educational disadvantages, his outlook on life was always positive. He took life in stride and retained his insatiable thirst for knowledge his entire life. I introduced Juan to a network marketing opportunity around 1996. A major component of this company was the interpersonal development of its distributors. We were all encouraged to listen to a motivational tape each week and read a new book every month. Many people read them.

Juan devoured them.

After a year or so he had developed a following of nearly 100 distributors and was making a bit of money. Like most people that become involved in multi-level marketing, his business started with a bang and ended with a whimper. Within 3 years, most of his volume and downline had vanished.

Juan was not a Harvard MBA. He didn't go to college and he wasn't an athlete. He didn't write a book and his name will not grace the façade of a university building. However, one of Juan's downline was a man by the name of Ramiro Armenta. When Juan's business dissolved, Ramiro and his small group also left and joined another company. The impact Juan had instilled in Ramiro was not in vain. In fact, Ramiro was personally responsible for about 80% of Juan's business. Juan had done what most people aren't willing to do or aren't able to do. He found and developed a person who was able to lead better than most.

A leader creates other leaders.

A great leader creates leaders with superior skills.

In a MLM or any business, many people climb the corporate ladder on the backs of their subordinates. True leadership has nothing to do with using people or "splitting commissions." True leadership never takes credit. True leaders create, embrace, train and encourage other leaders.

Juan Ramirez was a great leader.

As I sit here and write the final words to this book, it is the night before Juan's funeral. He died just 2 days ago and left behind 4 children, a wife, a mortgage and a hole in the universe. Fortunately, he also left behind his enthusiasm, attitude and gift for leadership. He placed these qualities in the capable hands of Ramiro Armenta.

You see, Ramiro has been steadily working his new business for years. In fact, his new enterprise is exploding. Ramiro Armenta's name is one that approaches near celebrity status in his industry. From dish washer to millionaire, he has impacted the lives of thousands of people and created financial independence for hundreds. At 36 years old, he is destined to increase that exponentially.

Without Juan, however, Ramiro might still be a dishwasher in Addison, IL. Fortunately for thousands of people, Ramiro took a liking to Juan and because of their friendship and Ramiro's influence; thousands of people will have financial security for the rest of their lives.

A butterfly flapped its wings. Thank you, Juan.

The Butterfly Effect is proof positive that what we do now – the actions we take today – have a profound and lasting impact on people and events that come in the future. What we do right here – *right now* – has important ramifications for not only our own future but also the future of generations to come. Everyone we come into contact with has the potential to strike the Butterfly Effect – and everyone's thoughts, actions and interactions determine the outcome of the future.

Dreaming big has its advantages. So does dreaming small. The only difference is the time you allow for your dream to spread, multiply and take hold.

Janice and Juan both have the butterfly effect as their legacy for greatness. What legacy will you leave behind?

Failure, regret, inaction or mediocrity is prohibitively more expensive then the toll required for your Express Lane to Success. Your life WILL touch the thousands of people who come in and go out of your life. The thoughts, actions and interactions you create will reverberate in the universe long after you are gone. Making good choices is only the beginning. Now is the time to create an abundant life full of health, wealth and prosperity.

You will be creating not only a full and rich life for yourself, but for your community and the world. The thoughts, actions and interactions you create will shape the destiny of the world.

Think. Better.

Act. Smarter.

Give. More.

Bexsi
You. Better.

~~Conclusion~~ Beginning

This is only a book.

However, with YOUR untapped potential, the combined forces of this book and your dream have the power to change your world and the world we all live in. You have a clear path to achieve whatever you want. You now have all the necessary tools to succeed. Not only to benefit yourself, but your family, your community and the world.

You've finished the reading portion. Have you interacted with the online portion?

You are already in one of three categories. The ACTION of circling a category and committing to the new you will create a chemical release in your body. A very small amount of endorphins will be released the moment you get out a pen and circle the category that best describes you.

What you do with that small amount of energy is up to you.

A butterfly flaps its wings.

Category A

Congratulations! You've read every single word in this book. You've gone online and finished every chapter. You filled out every single question honestly and thoroughly and you're about to have your own book delivered back to you because you're no longer the reader of success, you're the author of your own success. Your Bexsi™ system is in motion. You will be receiving a customized version of this book that reads like you wrote it...because you did.

Your ongoing reinforcement of motivation, inspiration, knowledge, awareness has begun. Your past failures are behind you and the new network you are part of will make you a terrific example for others.

Category B

You've skimmed over some of this book. You've read it. You're not consistent. You've read parts of it. You may have gone online and peeked at some of the end chapters and may be filled a question or two but you didn't really go through, in order, thoroughly and completely.

There's still hope for you.

There are new ideas or old ideas re-framed that are important to your success. If you use any one of these, you might still be successful but you face more challenges the longer you take and the more inconsistent you are. I'm sure you'd like to do this goal of yours in less time and with less pain, with a lot more energy and a lot more fun. So, I encourage you to go back and finish it and to look at every single line and every single word, fill out every single question and complete it, because it will work for you.

Category C

You didn't go online at all. You took this book and glanced over, maybe read a few chapters and felt, "Wow, I've heard this before. This is nice. This is good. I am motivated. That's all I need."

I've got bad news for you because I want you to go watch the movie, "The Karate Kid." If you are too lazy to do that, let me sum it up for you:

Daniel-san got the crap beaten out of him because he thought he knew karate. He got beat up because he *read* karate from a book. As the wise karate master, Mr. Miyagi said, "No Daniel-san. You can't learn karate from a book."

This book does not work all by itself.

This book only works when you work it. At a minimum it requires you to APPLY the principles. The more you put in place the support for your goals, the faster and more likely they will become your new reality. You still have a chance to succeed. If you do not go online, your chances are slim.

Category D

If you skimmed this, didn't read it at all or just went to end of the book to see how it concluded then go to the section on patience!

I don't mean to be rude, but this may not the right time for you. You have not created enough desire in your life. You don't have the passion to succeed like other people do. You don't have an ounce of self-esteem left. You had no energy. You have no commitment and therefore you have no chance right now of succeeding.

Reflect and think about what you want. And when the time is right for you, don't forget to pick this book up and look at it again. That's one of the magical characteristics about a book. When you read a really good novel, you just can't wait to turn that page you are engrossed in the process. You can't wait to see what happens next.

Books are timeless because you can go back, pick it up later and recreate that same, page-turning excitement. The energy and passion, the story and the emotion is all still there – ready, willing and able to engage you whenever you open it up.

If this is not the right time for you, that's OK. This may not be the perfect time to re-start your life.

When will that time come for you?

What will have to happen in order for you to take one small step for yourself?

What are you in control of, in order to take the next step?

I will be waiting for you to come on board and help you with your goal, your family and to change the world. Because of all the people out there who need to hear your story, there are at least two people who need to hear it quickly. And one of those people is you.

We have shamelessly plugged our accountability system throughout this book. It has been shameless because I believe in the butterfly effect, too.

My mission is to leave this world better then I found it. Your capacity to create a boundless life of prosperity is within you. It is my responsibility to reach out to YOU and extend a hand. This book may be our first meeting. I hope it has been a productive one.

Come on board as a fan, member or as a beacon of hope for others by joining our fellowship of achievement at www.bexsi.org. There is a lane open for you on our Express Lane to Success. Turn the key and put your foot on the gas. Your life can be anything you want it to be.

Bexsi
You. Better.

Books on Wisdom

The Wisdom of James Allen	James Allen
Seven Pillars of Wisdom	T. E. Lawrence
The Little Engine that Could	George Hauman
How to Win Friends and Influence People	Dale Carnegie
The little prince	Antoine Exupery

Books on Prosperity

One Minute Millionaire	Hansen/Allen
Cash in a Flash	Hansen/Allen
The Magic of Thinking Big	David Schwartz
The Richest Man in Babylon	George Clason
Millionaire Next Door	Stanley/Danko

Books on Success

You Were Born Rich	Bob Proctor
Endless Referrals	Bob Burg
Think and Grow Rich	Napoleon Hill
The Tipping Point	Malcolm Gladwell
7 Habits of Highly Effective People	Steven Covey

Inspirational Movies

1. IT'S A WONDERFUL LIFE 1946
2. STAND AND DELIVER 1988
3. SCHINDLER'S LIST 1993
4. ROCKY 1976
5. MR. SMITH GOES TO WASHINGTON 1939
6. E.T. THE EXTRA-TERRESTRIAL 1982
7. BREAKING AWAY 1979
8. SAVING PRIVATE RYAN 1998
9. APOLLO 13 1995
10. HOOSIERS 1986
11. ERIN BROCKOVICH 2000
14. THE DIARY OF ANNE FRANK 1959
12. THE RIGHT STUFF 1983
13. PAY IT FORWARD 2001
14. THE SECRET 2006
15. OCTOBER SKY 1999
16. THE SHAWSHANK REDEMPTION 1994
17. FIELD OF DREAMS 1989
18. GANDHI 1982
19. LAWRENCE OF ARABIA 1962
20. GLORY 1989
21. RUDY 1994